Copyright: L.B. McKenzie 2025

Contents

CHAPTER 1 — Sweet Potato Pudding 4

.... 18

Chapter 2, Death Preparations 19

Chapter 3 — Do Children Kill? 29

.... 47

Chapter 4 — Harvesting 48

Chapter 5 — World Within 58

Chapter 6 – Healing with Earth & Time 67

CHAPTER 7, No Family Secret 80

.... 96

Chapter 8 – Appreciation of Life 97

Chapter 9 – Love With Earth & Time 126

By: Olga Foreign   Conversations with My Grandfather

CHAPTER 1 — Sweet Potato Pudding

The sun had begun its slow descent into the horizon, casting a golden glow over the sprawling yard. The day had been full of celebration—laughter echoing through the halls of the family homestead, the smells of hearty food wafting from the kitchen, and the bustling of family members who had gathered for Agustus graduation. The older generations sat around the long wooden table in the Great Hall, savoring the last bites of lunch and catching up on the years that had passed. The younger ones were now dispersed, scattered across the backyard and fields, their voices rising in playful chatter and the soft rustle of children running through the grass.

It was a familiar scene, a routine so deeply ingrained in Lorna's bones that it felt almost like a tradition of its own. Every year, on these milestone occasions, the family would come together to celebrate and honor the moments of life they had shared. And this graduation weekend was no different. Today, Agustus, her son, graduated from college. He was 24 now, standing on the edge of adulthood, the promise of his future stretching before him. As she looked over at him talking to his cousins, she felt both a pang of pride and a quiet sadness, her boy had grown into a man.

After lunch, the air seemed to shift; the clinking of dishes and the hum of conversation faded into a more peaceful stillness. The children, still full of energy from the excitement, now meandered back to the shade of the old cotton tree, the same place where Lorna herself had sat many years ago. The cotton tree had stood witness to countless family gatherings, always providing a place of comfort, shelter, and quiet reflection.

Lorna, carrying a book, walked beneath the towering cotton tree, its wide, twisting branches casting a shadow over the gathering. The tree had been there as long as she could remember; its roots deeply embedded in the earth, like the roots of the family it shaded. The same cotton tree where her Grandparents had sat and shared stories with her as a child, now serving as a backdrop for her own storytelling to the next generation.

The Grandparents' house, now hers, stood just beyond the yard, solid and unyielding, the same one she had grown up in. She had inherited the property after their passing, feeling far too tied to it to leave. The house was filled with memories, every room whispering stories of her childhood, of lessons learned under the watchful eyes of Grandma and Grandpa, of moments that shaped the woman she had become. She was chosen by the elders to be the storyteller for this gathering. A positioned she took very seriously enough, to have written down several stories in the book she now clutches tightly in her hand. Yes, she could easily recount these stories from memory but, she wanted to ensure her memories were correct. So, for the last two months Lorna wrote, edited, and verified stories, to make this storytelling gathering as she remembered hers, right here, under the tree, listening to her Grandparents.

"Gather 'round, children," she said with a smile, her voice warm, rich with memory. "I'm going to tell you some stories. Stories of when I was your age, of my Grandparents, of the lessons they taught me that I carry with me every day."

Lorna turned her attention to the younger children of the family who had gathered around her, their faces eager, their eyes wide with curiosity as they sat cross-legged in the grass beneath the old cotton tree. Her heart swelled with the familiar pull of family, the kind of pull that had always kept her here, rooted to this land.

Lorna sat down on the soft grass beneath its wide branches, brushing her hands against the blades of green, feeling the warmth of the afternoon sun mixed with the coolness of the shade. The big cotton tree seemed to grow taller with every passing year, its massive trunk splitting into thick branches that stretched out like arms, cradling the land below. The children—her nieces, nephews, and cousins—gathered around her, eager and wide-eyed. It wasn't long before the younger ones, some barely old enough to remember much from last year's gathering, took their places on the grass at her feet, waiting for the stories to begin.

Their attention turned fully to her, and for a moment, she was back there again—sitting at her Grandparents' feet, listening to their stories. She could almost hear Grandma's soft voice, feel Grandpa's steady presence, and smell the sweet air of summers long past.

"Well, children," Lorna began, her voice carrying softly over the stillness of the afternoon, "it's a tradition, isn't it? To share the stories of our family when we gather like this."

They all nodded eagerly, some children shifting closer, others crossing their legs on the ground.

"I used to sit right where you are," she said, looking around at them. "Under this very tree, listening to your great-Grandparents' stories. You see, this tree—this house—it's all a part of our history, and it's important to remember where we come from."

This story is about Grandpa's Earth Oven and Grandma's Sweet Potato Pudding. Like the one we had today, wasn't that delicious? Your great grandmother Agnus did not have a kitchen like we do today, so this pudding was an all, day event that made it even more delicious. Lorna placed her glasses on her face, opened her book and started to read.

I was about seven years old, playing in the backyard, and bursting with annoying excitement. Today was the day, my grandpa was going to build an earth oven, out of mud and stone, while Grandma mixed up our favorite dessert, sweet potato pudding. Early in the morning, the neighbors all helped my grandfather gather the materials to build the oven. I did my best not to get in their way even though I must have asked a hundred questions. I remember Grandpa's hands, strong and sure, scooping up red clay soil to make the oven. He cleared a patch of ground early that morning and laid down a circle of old bricks and stones as a foundation. I watched wide-eyed as he added things like broken coconut shells and straw, packing mud and clay all around them to form a little dome. The dome oven had two openings: a small door in front where we could put in wood and food, and a tiny vent at the back to let out smoke and remove ashes. As the sun climbed higher, the clay dome dried and hardened. Grandpa even let me pat the cool damp clay with my palms, my fingers squishing in the mud. I giggled as bits of clay splattered on my legs; I felt like I was helping to build something amazing.

While Grandpa built the oven, he told me stories of how people long ago cooked in a similar way. *"Before we had stoves or electricity,"* he said, *"folks used ovens made from earth. Our ancestors baked bread in clay ovens that the whole village shared, many roasted foods in pits in the ground."* I could hardly imagine it, but he explained that using a communal oven – one shared by everyone – was common in villages all over the world for centuries. In those days, families would prepare their dough or dishes at home and then bring them to a big public oven to bake, while neighbors gathered around to chat and tell stories. I loved the way Grandpa described it: an oven not just for cooking, but for bringing people together. I didn't fully understand then, but I sensed that *our* day was going to bring everyone together too.

By late morning, the little mud oven was finished. Grandpa placed dry wood inside through the front opening and lit a fire. I jumped at the initial *whoosh* of flame, but soon the fire was crackling gently. Orange flames licked the inner walls of the clay oven, and thin blue smoke curled up through the vent. The smell of woodsmoke began to drift through the yard. Grandpa fed the fire until the clay was "good and fire-hot," as he put it. Once the inside was blazing, he let the flames die down. Then he used a long green branch with leaves, a makeshift broom, to sweep out the glowing charcoal and ash from inside the dome. The oven was now preheated and ready for baking, holding heat in its thick earthen walls. I bounced between Grandma's and Grandpa's side all morning, leaving only to satisfy my curiosity of what the other was doing

While Grandpa was busy outside, Grandma was in the kitchen (which was really just an outdoor shed) preparing the pudding. This wasn't any ordinary cake, it was the famous Grandma sweet potato pudding, a recipe passed down through generations. I dragged a stool over to watch her work. She had a big enamel basin in front of her and the entire area smelled like spices.

Grandma had peeled a pile of sweet potatoes, the kind with reddish skin and pale flesh, a lightish yellow yam. She grated them by hand on a metal grater, her arms moving rhythmically. I saw the mound of grated potato grow fluffy and moist in the basin. Grandpa had cracked open two dried coconuts with a cutlass and asked me to take them to Mrs. Mousa to be grated. I brought back the firm white coconut meat and watched, as my grandmother mixed it with water and then, squeezed it in a cloth to make rich coconut milk. Into the basin went cups of that creamy coconut milk, followed by heaping scoops of brown sugar that glistened like wet sand. Grandma added a handful of raisins (plump from soaking in a little rum), a pinch of salt, and plenty of spices, grated nutmeg, a bit of cinnamon and allspice. The warm aroma of those spices hit my nose, and I closed my eyes sniffing happily. She poured in a capful of real vanilla, and even a splash of rum for good measure (just enough to deepen the flavor, she said with a wink). Finally, she sprinkled in some flour and cornmeal to bind everything together.

With steady hands, Grandma stirred the mixture with a large wooden spoon. *Glup, glup,* went the batter, thick and molasses, brown, as she mixed in all the ingredients. Now and then she let me have a turn at stirring – it was heavy work for my small arms, but I loved seeing the raisins pop up here and there and the ribbons of grated sweet potato swirled in the mix. The batter was lumpy and hearty, not smooth like a cake batter, because of all the grated ingredients. When Grandma lifted the spoon, the mixture fell back into the bowl with a splat.

Grandma greased a deep cast iron Dutch pot with butter and then poured the sweet potato mixture in. I watched as she dotted the top with a few small pieces of margarine and covered the pot with its heavy iron lid. The batter was so thick that tapping the pot hardly made a jiggle. She set it aside to rest a bit while Grandpa got the oven ready. I could barely contain myself, hovering around and asking, *"Is it time to put it in yet?"* Grandma shooed me outside with a grin, telling me to go see how Grandpa was doing – likely because I was getting too underfoot in my excitement. I announced loudly to Grandpa that the pudding was ready from the window. He came into the kitchen, hugged my grandmother's waist and, then carried the Dutch pot with the pudding outside to the oven. I stayed with Grandma to help her clean up the kitchen until I inadvertently created a mess and was shooed away.

I skipped back outside and, found Grandpa checking the heat of the earth oven by tossing a bit of cornmeal inside to see if it toasted. Satisfied, he carefully lifted the heavy pot with the pudding batter and slid it into the oven. He then sealed the opening with a metal sheet. For extra measure, he shoveled a few hot coals on top of the metal sheet and around the sides – truly baking it from above and below, just like in the old days. *"Fire a top, fire a bottom, yum yum in the middle!"* Grandpa chuckled. The pudding was in the best place, surrounded by heat so it would cook evenly. Traditionally it's cooked with fire on top and fire below, making the pudding hot on both ends and heavenly in the center. I didn't fully grasp the words then, but I sure understood that *yum yum in the middle* meant something delicious was coming out of that oven! I gave a little happy dance right there, anticipating the sweet, spiced "yum yum" that would soon be on my tongue.

With the pudding safely baking, now came the hardest part, waiting. See children it's not like today where things are instantaneous. Back then you had to wait, but the waiting was usually always worth it. While we waited, Grandpa raked some of the extra coals under a nearby iron griddle to roast cashews, peanuts and yams from the neighbors (no heat goes to waste in our yard). I sat on a low stool by the oven's mouth, smelling the mingling scents of wood smoke and the sweet potato pudding slowly cooking. The heavy fragrance of coconut milk and brown sugar began to sneak out, making the air smell like caramel and toasted nuts. Every now and then a whiff of allspice and nutmeg would drift by, as the pudding set, and its top started to crust slightly. My stomach growled loudly, which made Grandpa laugh, *"Little miss greedy,* Patience." I pouted a bit, but then he started telling stories to pass the time.

As we waited, Grandpa told me more about why he built this oven. He explained that an earth oven like ours was not just for our family in the past it was for the whole community. In some villages, everyone would gather when the oven was fired. *"Many hands build the oven, and many mouths get to share the food,"* he said. I imagined how, long ago, perhaps my great, great, Grandparents in a mountain village baked like this, with neighbors helping each other. Where a baker would fire up a big clay oven and the whole town comes by with their dough to bake fresh bread. I could almost see it: rows of golden loaves wrapped in leaves, villagers drawn in by the smell, lining up with big smiles. The communal oven would be the heart of those gatherings, everyone talking, laughing, swapping stories while the bread loaves baked.

He even told me of a saying from across the ocean: *"The earth is an oven"*, meaning the earth itself gives us the fire and warmth to bake and live. As a child, I didn't entirely follow Grandpa's sayings, but I felt the meaning in my belly – food tastes better when many people make it and enjoy it together.

Before I knew it, an hour or two had passed. Grandma checked the pudding by carefully lifting the lid a crack (using a folded cloth to shield her from the heat). The moment that lid opened, a wave of incredible aroma hit us – sweet potatoes, spice, and coconut, all mingled and perfect. The pudding had a firm, browned crust at the edges and a slightly soft center that quivered gently. *"The top is still a little soft, just how it's supposed to be,"* Grandma murmured with satisfaction. A soft custardy layer on the very top, is the best part Grandpa firmly announced. She took a spoon and lightly drizzled a mixture of dark rum and lime juice over the pudding, a traditional finishing touch that seeped down creating glossy sweet pockets in the crust. This rum mixture was delivered by Mr. Tang, who arrived just in time, to help Grandpa remove the roasted nuts from the oven. I bounced on my toes as Grandpa pulled the pot out of the oven with thick mitts. *It was finally ready!*

By now, the delicious smell had worked its magic on more than just me. I saw a couple of neighborhood women peeking over the fence, and soon they wandered over, drawn by the scent of the pudding. The nearby children had also gathered, eyes wide and noses in the air. We didn't have to call anyone; the aroma was an open invitation. Grandpa always says, *"Food smell has foot,"* meaning the scent will travel far and bring people in. And indeed, here they came! Before I realized it, a little crowd formed under the cotton tree in our yard. Laughter and chatter rose up, everyone was saying *"Agnus bake pudding today?"*, *"Yes, come taste!"* Grandma began slicing up the pudding right there in the iron pot, steam rising as each square piece came out. The insides were creamy and moist, studded with plump raisins, and the top was sticky, soft and glistening. It was as if all the sweetness of love was baked into that pudding, the earth that grew the sweet potatoes, the coconuts from the palm, the sugar from cane fields, the spices from the hills. Everything had come together in this one dish, in this one moment.

Children I confess, for a moment, I squeezed in next to Grandma and thought, *maybe if I stay here, I can get the biggest piece… maybe even keep some just for us.* I was a little girl, and that greedy thought flashed in my mind when I saw so many people wanting a taste of *my* grandma's pudding. The first slice went to old Miss Enid from two houses down, the next to Mr. Brown the tailor… I grew nervous that my share would be too small. Sensing my hesitation, Grandpa put his arm around my shoulder and bent down to speak softly in my ear. *"Lorna,"* he said, *"many work together, therefore, many shall play, eat, sing, and dance together."* That was his gentle reminder that because everyone had helped; whether gathering wood, building the oven, or even just sharing in the excitement, everyone deserved to enjoy the reward. I looked around at the smiling faces: my schoolmates who helped pick sweet potatoes, our neighbors who lent a hand by bringing over extra firewood, and even the ones who simply cheered us on. I realized the whole day had been a group effort. Grandpa's wise words melted the selfishness right out of me. I nodded up at him with a small smile.

At last, it was *my* turn to get a slice. Grandma handed it to me on a fresh green banana leaf. It was warm to the touch, and I could see the creamy middle of the pudding wobble just a bit, loaded with raisins and scented with nutmeg. I took a big bite, pure heaven. The texture was dense pudding-like, not fluffy like cake but smooth and hearty. The taste? Better than I even dreamed: sweet and spiced, with the mellow richness of sweet potato and coconut and a hint of smoky flavor from the wood fire. Truly, as Grandpa had joked, *"yum yum in the middle"* a joyful chorus of flavors in my mouth. I think I might have even closed my eyes in bliss. Around me, I heard murmurings of delight as others savored their portions. Miss Enid licked her fingers and proclaimed it the best she'd had in years. The children scraped their banana leaves for every last bit.

With everyone enjoying the pudding, someone pulled out a drum –to play kumina rhythms. Another neighbor began clapping a steady beat. Before long, we had music and singing under the cotton tree. With sticky, sweet mouths, we children started to dance, our laughter ringing out. The adults clapped and swayed, humming old folk songs. The whole yard turned into a little celebration. The clay oven, still warm and glowing, stood by quietly as a proud centerpiece of our gathering. In the golden afternoon light, with the smell of sweet potato pudding still in the air, we truly lived the spirit of Grandpa's words, *"many had worked together, and now many were rejoicing together."*

I share this story with you little ones as that day left a warm glow in my memory. I learned that food is more than just something to fill my belly – it's something that can bring people together. I learned how our sweet potato pudding carries history in it: from our ancestors who brought their methods of communal cooking, to my very own Grandparents who showed me how to blend all that tradition with love and share it freely. And now, as I tell you this tale, I feel as if the sweet taste of that pudding and the sound of our family's laughter are alive again under this cotton tree.

So, little ones, whenever you smell something delicious cooking, remember: it's an invitation. It might be calling you to help, to learn, or just to be with others. And when we all work together, whether building an oven, grating potatoes, or even just gathering to listen to a story, we will all play together, eat together, sing and dance together. That is the real magic, the true "family," in the middle of everything.

Lorna paused. The story flowed from her as though it had been waiting to be told, but now, as she looked at her son, a new realization washed over her. The stories she was sharing weren't just memories, they were lessons. Lessons on family, on love, on the strength of their heritage.

"Your great Grandpa and great Grandma taught me that family is not just about blood," she said, her voice softening. "It's about love, respect, and the things we pass down. They didn't just teach me with their words; they taught me with their actions. Every meal they made, every song they sang, every evening spent together—that was a lesson in what it means to be a part of something bigger than yourself."

The air grew cooler as evening fell. Lorna listened to the children talk amongst themselves about their sweet potato pudding moments, and smiled. She wondered if any of them would ever get to see an earth oven being built and wonder if she could have one built for the next gathering. It was time for the next story before dinner and chores. Lorna, settled the children around her, the first story filled with nostalgia, the next may bring some sadness but, should be shared based on the events anticipated to occur within the next few years. With the youngest elder being me and the oldest ninety, eight years old, there will be a series of death in our family's immediate future.

By: Olga Foreign   Conversations with My Grandfather

Chapter 2, Death Preparations

As not to lose the children's attention Lorna asked the question, Children do you know I was raised with a donkey? True, very true. Lorna placed her glasses on her face, opened the book and started to read.

Wishes was the name of my grandfather's donkey. We grew up together or, at least that's what I thought. When I was about to turn eighteen, looking forward to graduation and college; I couldn't help but notice how much Wishes had changed. His once, glossy coat had lost its shine, now speckled with gray hairs, and his gait had become slower, more deliberate, as if every step took more effort than the last. He seemed so much older than I remembered.

Wishes had a sturdy frame, though his once vibrant chestnut fur was fading into a muted brown, peppered with patches of gray and white. His long ears drooped slightly now, though they used to perk up at every sound, especially when he was excited or in a playful mood. The scent of hay and the soft musk of his coat filled the air whenever he was near. His thick, long mane was matted in places, as if he could no longer keep up with the grooming he once enjoyed. His tail flicked lazily, and his once, sparkling eyes now appeared tired, their warmth dimming with the passing of years.

I noticed that my grandfather was gentler with him, seldom riding him anymore. Still, he took Wishes on the same daily trek, as if it were important for Wishes to remember how to walk and visit the familiar places they had always explored together. I'd watch them from the window, seeing the old man's hand resting lightly on the donkey's side, a silent gesture of connection. They were like two old friends; the years shared in comfortable companionship.

One afternoon, I saw Grandpa sitting on the porch, carving a piece of wood from a tree trunk. His large, weathered hands moved with precision, the steady scraping of the knife filling the quiet air. I still remember the smell of fresh wood shavings mixed with the scent of the earth, rich and fertile, as the summer sun beat down softly. Grandpa was making a plaque, his face focused, lost in the simple task. When he finished, he started chiseling the word "Wishes" onto the wood, his hands working carefully and thoughtfully, smoothing out the letters as if the donkey's name deserved the most respect.

Then he looked up at me, a slight smile on his lips. "Anything you want to put here?"

"Why?" I asked, my brow furrowed in confusion.

He smiled faintly; his eyes soft yet knowing. "Wishes will understand. Whatever you want to put here."

For a moment, I thought it was silly—thinking that Wishes could read. I was almost eighteen, after all. Still, I hesitated, my mind swirling with thoughts. Finally, I said softly, "Your wish has come true." Grandpa chiseled the words into the plaque with careful strokes, adding the year beneath it.

At eighteen, I felt the weight of transition pressing upon me. My body had filled out, my once girlish frame now more defined with curves I hadn't fully accepted yet. I had grown taller, my legs longer and leaner, but I still caught myself looking in the mirror, unsure of how I felt about the changes.

And yet, no matter how much I had grown, there was still something in me that felt like a child, a child trying to hold on to the fleeting moments of a life I knew was changing.

The following week, I saw Grandpa and Mr. Mousa walking into the backyard, carrying shovels. They began digging a hole in the soft earth. From the kitchen window, I watched them, as I stood beside my grandmother, my curiosity piqued but uncertain. There was a sense of finality in their actions. They covered the bottom of the hole with large banana leaves, vibrant with life, and then placed flowers and herbs on top. The colors were so bright, so alive, contrasting sharply with the heaviness of the moment. Once the hole was ready, they placed a tarp over it and walked together towards Mr. Mousa's yard.

I didn't want to go to my grandpa as I thought this was one of those moments. Grandpa always said that sometimes men needed time alone.

I turned to my grandmother, who was baking bread, her hands working skillfully through the dough. The loaves that were already baking filled the air with comfort and familiarity. "What are they doing?" I asked, my voice barely above a whisper.

She paused, looking up at me with soft eyes. "Death preparations," she said, her voice gentle, but there was a weight behind her words. It wasn't just a fact, it was a lesson, an acknowledgment of the life that was coming to an end.

"Who's dying?" I whispered, the words heavy in my chest.

She paused for a moment, and then her face softened with a sadness that I hadn't expected. "Wishes."

My heart dropped. I couldn't speak. The air around me seemed to grow still as I walked out the kitchen door, my legs moving almost by instinct. I ran to Wishes, wrapping my arms around his neck, feeling the roughness of his fur beneath my fingers. Tears streamed down my face as I whispered, "What's wrong with you? Why do they think you're dying? Don't leave, Wishes." His familiar scent, the musky earthiness of his coat mixed with the sweetness of the grass he ate, filled my senses.

Grandma came out and hugged me, her warmth a steady comfort as I clung to Wishes. "He's tired," she said softly. "He's tired of standing, tired of chewing, tired of walking. He's done a good job while he's been with us. You love him, and he loves you. But we all have our time, and his time is coming soon."

She handed me a brush, its wooden handle smooth in my hand, and held my hand as I gently brushed Wishes' mane, the strands soft and slightly frayed from years of wear. I cried, knowing that outside of my Grandparents, he was the only other family member I saw almost every day. He had been my companion through so many of my childhood memories, the constant presence in the background of my life.

The following Monday, Grandpa asked if I wanted to stay home from school that day. With a somber tone, I replied, "Yes, if I have to," then laughed, though it was a laugh tinged with sadness. After breakfast, Grandpa asked if I would go with him to collect Wishes' favorite foods. I happily grabbed the basket and ran over to Wishes, whispering in his ear, "Grandpa will make you healthy again. He's going to treat you with food medicine like he did before. Hang in there, Wishes."

We gathered white sugar cane, wild onions, sweet lemongrass, almonds, and sweet potato roots. The sweetness of the sugar cane was still fresh in my mind as we washed them together. Grandpa then filled Wishes' trough with water, adding a bit of rum to the mixture. I couldn't help but laugh as I stirred the brew, remembering how much Wishes loved rum.

When Grandpa left, I stayed with Wishes, recounting old stories of the fun times we had together. I remembered the day I tried to make Wishes swim with me on his back across the river to the other bank, but he refused for hours, stubbornly staying put on the riverbank. Instead, Wishes nudged me back home forcefully, like a mother hen protecting her young, and I was convinced he had tattled on me to Grandma. Back then, I swore that Wishes could talk.

That evening, Grandpa sat with me on the porch. We watched Wishes standing quietly by the fence, chewing slowly, as the sunset painted the sky in hues of orange and pink, the light shifting across the land like a soft, gentle touch. Grandpa put his hand on my shoulder; his weathered fingers warm against my skin. "You know, he's had a long, good life," he said, his voice soft but steady. "Sometimes the best thing we can do for those we love is to let them go when they're ready."

I wiped my eyes and nodded, though my heart wasn't ready to accept it. We stayed there until the sky darkened, telling stories of Wishes, how he used to kick over Grandpa's tools when he didn't get his favorite treat, and how he would bray loudly every morning to wake the chickens. In those stories, Wishes seemed ageless, forever lively and spirited.

That night, I sat by Wishes' side, humming softly as he lay down. For the first time, I noticed how slow his breathing had become, how his once vibrant eyes were now dull and tired. I whispered, "I love you, Wishes," and I stayed with him until sleep finally took me too.

The next morning, Grandpa woke me gently, his face somber. "He's gone," he whispered.

We prepared for the funeral that day. Grandpa placed the plaque we had made at the head of the grave, and we gathered flowers from the garden. Mr. Mousa came over to help, and a few neighbors joined us. Grandma brought a small bouquet of wildflowers and laid it beside the plaque.

Standing there, I couldn't stop the tears. Grandpa patted my shoulder as he spoke softly about Wishes, sharing stories of his strength, loyalty, and gentle spirit. I couldn't bring myself to speak, but I felt grateful to have loved him.

When it was time, Grandpa placed a handful of earth over the grave, and I did the same. As the sun dipped below the horizon, we finished covering the grave with soil, placing the flowers and the plaque on top. I read the plaque again: "Wishes, Your Wish Has Come True" and the date. I ran my hand over the carved words and looked at my grandfather. At the time I spoke those words, I didn't know Wishes was dying.

My grandfather pulled me into his arms, placing a hand on each of my cheeks. He looked me in the eye and said, "When we think of each other with love, the right words will always flow at the right moment. Wishes understands what you meant, and you were right, he always wanted to be a lazy, loved, and carefree donkey. That was the life I gave him in exchange for some small favors like rides and help with heavy loads. He loved guarding you and watching you grow."

We stood in silence, listening to the evening sounds, and I felt a profound emptiness. I whispered one last time, "Goodbye, Wishes."

The memory of Wishes lingered, as all the losses in our family seemed to do, but it was different now. Time had softened the edges of that sorrow, leaving only the faintest trace behind. I was no longer the child running behind my grandfather, needing his comforting presence in the face of death.

After finishing the somber story of her grandfather's donkey, Lorna took a deep breath and smiled gently at the children, her eyes softening. "Remember children your great Grandpa's words "When we think of each other with love, the right words will always flow at the right moment." Now, I think it's time we all head inside for dinner, as it's getting a bit chilly out here. Who's ready for some goat stew and fresh, baked bread?" Her smile was a quiet invitation, and the children, sensing the shift, eagerly bounced to their feet, their laughter starting to bubble again as they hurried inside, the weight of sadness lifted, it was time for a taste of sweet life with food and family.

Chapter 3 — Do Children Kill?

As usual, the elders were awake first, rising early to greet the soft, golden light of another beautiful Saturday morning. The crisp air, infused with the scent of dew and earth, was refreshing as the village stirred to life. The sounds of roosters crowing echoed in the distance, and the hustle of the day began slowly, with each moment unfolding in harmony. Gradually, the rest of the family began to gather, emerging from their rooms as the sun climbed higher, some rubbing their eyes, others already eager for the day to begin.

Breakfast was always a family affair, one that required many hands, but it never felt like work. It was more of a ritual, a comforting dance of shared responsibilities. The children were quick to help, their small hands eagerly passing dishes, setting the table, and taking their places as the elders made their way to the grand dining room. Lorna watched with a smile on her face, the sight of the age dynamics, the wisdom of the elders and the uncontainable energy of the children, filling her with a sense of warmth and belonging. There was something deeply pleasing about seeing them all together, each generation playing its part, finding its place in the circle.

Once everyone had settled at the table, with the younger ones squirming with excitement and the elders quietly enjoying their meal, Lorna stood and announced with a twinkle in her eye, *"Story time will begin immediately after breakfast cleanup is completed, and I have three great and fun stories to share with all of you."*

A murmur of excitement spread through the room, and just as quickly, her father stood, ready to lend a hand. He was a man of action, always ready to jump in and assist wherever needed. Lorna nodded in appreciation, grateful for his help in organizing snacks, drinks, and keeping track of the children's eager energy. An elder was always needed to maintain some semblance of order, and her father was always up to the task. His presence was like a steady hand, guiding everything into place.

The meal wrapped up with the customary laughter, jokes, and friendly chatter. Plates were cleared, cups were refilled, and soon, the grand dining room was bustling with the cheerful noise of cleanup. As the last of the dishes were put away, the children, who had been eagerly whispering to each other about the stories to come, ran outside. One by one, they gathered beneath the shade of the great cotton tree, its sturdy branches stretching wide, offering shelter and comfort, the perfect place to settle for a full morning of stories.

Lorna watched them from the doorway for a moment, her heart full as she admired the unity of her family, both old and young, gathered together for this long-standing tradition. The air was thick with anticipation, and she could hear the murmur of voices as the children settled down, their faces lit with the excitement of the tales to come. Lorna sat down on the grass, pulled out her journal, placed her glasses on her face and began to read.

Every Saturday, my grandfather played dominoes with three of his lifelong friends. The game took place in the cozy living room of Mr. Tang's house, a room that had witnessed decades of camaraderie. The scent of aged mahogany furniture mixed with faint tobacco smoke and the sweet aroma of freshly baked treats. On the walls, black-and-white photographs of Mr. Tang's family lined the space, capturing moments from a time long passed. The floorboards creaked softly underfoot as the men made themselves comfortable in their chairs, and the low hum of the ceiling fan mingled with the occasional clink of dominoes being shuffled.

The room was dimly lit, with a single lamp casting a warm, golden glow over the table, where the dominoes would soon be played. The atmosphere was one of comfortable routine, with every corner of the room rich with memories. A window was cracked open, and through the delicate curtains, the scent of jasmine from the garden outside wafted in, mixing with the musky undertone of the room. The table at the center was the focal point, smooth, well, worn, and a little scratched from years of use, but sturdy and reliable, much like the men who gathered around it.

From the time I was five, I would beg my grandfather to take me along. His response was always the same: "Only if you behave and don't cause trouble." I would smile, both eager and anxious, as I slipped my small hand into his, feeling the roughness of his skin—a contrast to the softness of mine. Together, we would make our way down the dirt path to Mr. Tang's house, the sound of our footsteps faint beneath the rhythm of our shared anticipation.

Looking back, I now understand why he brought me. My grandfather was a man of few words but great pride. His broad, weathered face was a testament to his life of hard work and sacrifice. His eyes, dark, sharp, and always observing, held a certain wisdom that only years could bring. I was his pride and joy, his legacy, the proof that his sacrifices had not been in vain. Every week, he would proudly present me to his friends, almost as if to say, "Look at her. One of my offsprings has given me this tiny girl, a unique, thoughtful, fearless thinker."

As we entered, Mr. Tang, a man of Chinese descent, greeted us with a broad, welcoming smile, his dark eyes crinkling at the corners. He wore a simple linen shirt, sleeves rolled up as if ready for anything. His skin, a little lighter than my grandfather's, carried the stories of his ancestors, as did the furniture in his home. The scent of incense lingered in the air, mingling with the rich tones of tea being poured. Mr. Tang was always the one to start the conversation with a light-hearted joke, his deep voice steady and calm.

He handed me a carefully wrapped gift for my seventh birthday, which had passed just the day before. I thanked him politely, my fingers tracing the edges of the wrapping before I passed the gift over to my grandfather to unwrap. Inside, the room hummed with a gentle buzz of conversation, and the low clinking of glasses being filled with cool drinks.

In the corner, Mr. Mousa, a tall and imposing man from Kenya, sat with a glass of rum in his hand. His skin was deep brown, a rich shade that contrasted with the light wood of the room. His features were strong; his face etched with years of wisdom and laughter. He had a deep, booming voice that could fill the room effortlessly, and when he spoke, it was always with purpose. Mr. Katz, another friend of my grandfather's, was the quietest of the bunch, his face lined with years of thoughtfulness. He was German, with pale skin and soft, graying hair that seemed to match his calm demeanor. Though not as physically imposing as Mr. Mousa, his presence was just as important to the group—his sharp mind and gentle nature grounding the rest.

The table was set, and the dominoes were arranged in their familiar pattern. The game began as always, the rhythm of the game becoming the heartbeat of the room. The soft clink of the pieces against each other was the only sound for a few moments, aside from the murmur of the wind outside. The living room, still dimly lit by the single lamp, seemed to hold its breath as the game began in earnest. The conversation, which had slowed in anticipation, picked up again, each man speaking in turn, their voices low and comfortable, as though this moment had happened a thousand times before.

I pulled my small stool up to my grandfather's side glancing up at him with a mixture of admiration and awe. His weathered hands—rough from years of hard work and experience—moved with quiet precision as he rearranged his dominoes, the slight glint of his wedding band catching the light for a brief moment. His face, with its deep lines and high cheekbones, was a portrait of patience and wisdom, his dark eyes fixed on the game before him.

I, on the other hand, sat perched on my small stool, my legs swinging freely beneath me. It was an old, sturdy thing—paint chipped on the edges, the wood a faded brown from years of use. It was low enough for me to sit comfortably and watch the game unfold before me, though it always felt a little too big for my small frame. My legs swung freely beneath me, tapping lightly against the floor, my pigtails bouncing as I eagerly leaned forward to catch every moment of the conversation. I wore a simple cotton dress, the colors a bit faded from the sun, and my thick, dark hair was tied into two neat pigtails that swayed as I moved. My almond, shaped eyes were filled with curiosity as I watched the men play.

As always, the game's rhythm blended with the ease of their voices. I could feel the weight of the tradition, the years of friendship and shared stories hanging in the air like a familiar, comforting blanket. Mr. Tang, always the one to initiate the discussions, leaned back in his chair, his dark eyes twinkling as he looked around the table. His face, which was round and smooth with slight crow's feet at the corners of his eyes, seemed to hold an eternal youth beneath his age. His slow, deliberate gaze was a perfect complement to his calm demeanor.

"Whose turn is it to tell a tale of old?" my grandfather asked, his voice deep and steady as the game slowed momentarily.

"I will, Augustus," (my grandfather's name) replied Mr. Katz, the quiet German who always spoke in carefully considered tones. His hair, now graying at the temples, matched the warmth in his eyes, a warmth that spoke of a quiet, thoughtful life. He paused for a moment, looking around at us, his friends. The anticipation in the room was almost palpable as he prepared to begin.

"Tonight's story is *Who Killed the Cat?*" Mr. Katz's voice was low and mysterious, a perfect setup for the tale he was about to tell.

I leaned in closer, my heart beating a little faster, eager to hear what would happen next. The men were always so good at drawing out the suspense, at leaving you hanging on each word as the story unfolded. It was like magic, this way they had of making the simplest things seem so much more.

The room felt smaller now, more intimate. The warmth of the evening, the soft flicker of the lamp, and the smell of rich tea brewing in the corner added to the sense that this was a moment outside of time—a moment that belonged only to those gathered in that room. As Mr. Katz began, his voice took on a different tone, one that drew me in deeper. The storytelling was my favorite part, but it was the discussions afterward that truly captured my attention. As the dominoes were shuffled, Mr. Katz began his tale, his words flowing smoothly, pulling me into the mystery.

"In a house of ten, with five children among them, lived a three-generation family: a husband and wife, a grandmother and grandfather, and a granduncle."

His words began to paint the picture of a house—a modest home, nestled somewhere far away from the bustle of the city. The house was an old wooden structure, its edges softened by years of wear and tear. The floorboards groaned underfoot, and the smell of old dust mixed with the earthy scent of the garden outside. It was the kind of house that seemed to hold secrets within its walls, secrets that had been passed down like heirlooms. The high ceilings made the house feel large, but the cramped furniture, mismatched and worn from years of use, made the space feel smaller and more intimate. The family was always in motion, yet each seemed to live in their own world, their own space, connected but separate.

The children, each one a unique character in their own right, were the pulse of this home. They played in the backyard, their laughter filling the air as they chased each other through the tall grass. The grandfather, who was blind, lived in a world that was quiet but ever-present. His hearing was sharp, his mind even sharper. He sat at the head of the table, his senses honed by years of living in a world where sight no longer mattered. His touch was sensitive to the world around him. The room, though dark and dim, felt alive to him in a way it couldn't to the rest of them. His face, pale and deeply lined, seemed ageless, as though the years had washed over him but left his soul untouched. His wife, the grandmother, suffered from dementia, her memories fading like a mist that never quite lifted. She sat quietly, her frail frame seeming almost lost in the worn armchair that enveloped her. Her soft eyes, clouded with the fog of dementia, occasionally flickered with recognition, though she rarely spoke. And then there was the granduncle, a grumpy man who seemed to be perpetually annoyed with everyone and everything. A tall, angular, with a face that seemed to have been carved from stone, forever locked in a scowl. His voice, though deep, often carried a tinge of irritation, as though the world owed him something. He sat with his arms folded across his chest, a glass of something strong in front of him,

But it wasn't just the people who shaped this home. There was also a cat, a stray cat that had wandered into the yard one day and never left. The cat, with its disheveled fur and indifferent eyes, became part of the family in its own strange way. The children fed it, but no one really cared enough to give it a proper name. It was simply *Cat*, and that was enough for them.

The story Mr. Katz wove began to take shape in the minds of all who listened, his words painting a vivid image of a house that was both bustling and oppressive. The children, five in total, ranging from three to fourteen, brought an energy that was constant and chaotic, yet strangely melancholic in its own way.

As Mr. Katz spoke of the family, he described them with an eerie calm, his voice rising and falling like the swell of an ocean. "After Sunday morning breakfast, the mother would scrape the leftover food into the cat's bowl. She called out 'Cat' twice before walking away, continuing with her chores. The men, as usual, spent their time in the library, idle chatter filling the air as they tried to irritate one another, all while keeping an eye on the youngest child, who was easily appeased with a few dumplings."

I could see it in my mind—this household, full of sounds, yet oddly hushed, as if something was about to unfold but hadn't yet. The scent of food lingering in the air, the weight of quiet conversations, and the sound of a cat meowing lazily as it wandered through the yard.

"The children, all under the watchful eyes of their older siblings, went about their morning routine—chores and play, all blending together in the sun, drenched backyard. The three-year-old, often loud and insistent, would call for her grandpa, her voice shrill in its demands, yet always met with a sense of indifference by the older ones."

In my mind, I could picture the little girl, no older than I was at the time, running through the backyard, her pigtails bouncing as she demanded attention from everyone. I imagined the rough, sunbaked earth beneath her feet, the smell of ripe fruit from the trees that shaded the yard, and the soft rustling of the grass as she dashed between the cotton trees and around the wooden fence. The children's laughter and squabbles mixed together in a chaotic harmony, a symphony of innocence and disarray.

"Eventually," Mr. Katz continued, his voice dropping lower, "the cat had disappeared from its usual spots, and the children, eager to find it, began their search. They first checked the back porch, where the cat's food bowl was kept, but it was empty. They then searched under the cotton tree, where the cat often slept, but still no sign."

The air around us seemed to grow heavier, the weight of the story pressing in on me as I listened. The simple mystery of the missing cat felt like it would unravel something much deeper—something hidden within the family. My eyes remained locked on Mr. Katz as he spoke, his voice soft yet compelling, weaving a thread of unease throughout the room.

"Finally, they found the Cat, lying lifeless in the guest bathroom, a chopstick protruding from its ear."

The words hung in the air like an accusation. A gasp slipped from my lips before I could stop it. The room seemed to pause, and I could hear the faint rustling of Mr. Mousa's drink being set down on the table, his deep voice cutting through the silence.

"The children screamed, their voices rising in terror as they stumbled back from the scene," Mr. Katz continued. "And when the men arrived, they quickly moved the children out of the room, their faces grim as they stared at the scene before them. No one knew who had done it, but the question hung there, unspoken."

The heat in the room suddenly felt oppressive, and I could see the flickering shadows cast by the lamp grow long and distorted across the walls. The space felt crowded, as if every person there had become part of the story in some way, their lives woven into the tale.

Lunch was a somber affair. The grandmother wept quietly in the corner, her hands trembling as she clutched the edges of her shawl. The children barely ate, their eyes wide with confusion and fear, while the men spoke in hushed tones, trying to piece together what had happened. The cat, once so indifferent to them all, now lay in the silence of the bathroom, a victim of something no one had yet understood.

After lunch, the mood remained heavy. The silence at the table was deafening, broken only by the occasional scrape of a chair or the soft clink of glass. The men, normally animated and lively in their conversations, now sat in quiet contemplation, their faces serious. As the day stretched on, the adults retreated to the backyard, gathering under the shade of the old cotton tree. The tree stood tall and proud, its branches sweeping low, almost as if it were shielding them from the weight of the world. Its leaves rustled softly in the breeze, and the scent of earth and moss filled the air. Here, the men sat in a loose circle, their faces shaded but their minds far from at ease.

After dinner, a ceremony was held for the cat's burial, with only the mother offering a few words. The children's emotions fluctuated between tears and silence, while the adults consoled them before holding a brief meeting outside under the large cotton tree. The mother was the first to speak, her voice shrill and agitated as she demanded to know who had killed the cat and left it in the bathroom, lacking the sense to lock the door and prevent the children from discovering such a gruesome scene. In unison, everyone replied, "I didn't."

I stayed close to my grandfather, my eyes flicking from his calm expression to the rest of the group. I was too young to understand the gravity of the situation, but I knew enough to sense the tension hanging in the air. The adults murmured to one another, their voices low but urgent, their brows furrowed in concentration. I couldn't help but feel that something important was happening, something I didn't yet have the words for.

"Who killed the cat?" Mr. Mousa's voice broke the quiet, his deep, rich tone commanding attention. He leaned forward slightly, his large frame almost seeming to absorb the surrounding space. His dark skin gleamed in the light filtering through the leaves, and his deep-set eyes were intense as he spoke.

The question lingered in the air, unspoken but hanging between them all. It was as if everyone in the circle had already been assigned a role, and they were all waiting for the truth to be revealed.

Mr. Tang, always the pragmatic one, scratched his chin thoughtfully before speaking. "It must be the granduncle," he said, his voice calm but laced with suspicion. "He's always been grumpy. The cat likely annoyed him."

But my grandfather, always sharp and perceptive, shook his head. "That's too obvious," he said, his deep voice cutting through the tension. His eyes, though kind, were sharp, and there was something in them that suggested he saw more than others did.

"And the cause of death?" Mr. Mousa inquired, his voice low and skeptical. "A chopstick jabbed into its ear? That seems too vicious. I don't think it was the children or the women."

The air seemed to thicken as the men exchanged glances. It was as if they were all circling the truth, but no one dared to name it yet. The cat's death was no ordinary event; it was a mystery that had roots deeper than anyone realized. As the shadows lengthened and the sky turned from a soft blue to a rich, dusky purple, the men continued to deliberate, their voices low but steady.

I tugged at my grandfather's sleeve, my small fingers desperate to get his attention. He turned to me, his face softening when he saw the curiosity in my eyes.

"What is it, little one?" he asked gently, his voice a quiet anchor in the storm of conversation around us.

I hesitated, then whispered, "Do children kill?"

My grandfather's hand, large and worn, gently cupped my chin. He leaned down to look at me, his gaze steady and serious. "Yes," he said softly, "children can be efficient, unremorseful killers, acting without any logical reasoning."

I felt a chill run through me at his words, but I didn't pull away. There was something about the way he said it that made me think he wasn't just talking about the cat. There was something more—something hidden deep within the question, a part of life that I wasn't yet ready to understand, but would eventually come to know.

I raised my hand, just as I had been taught, waiting until Mr. Tang acknowledged me. When he did, I stood up and spoke, my voice trembling slightly as I pulled at my left hand's index finger.

"The three-year-old girl killed the cat," I said, my voice small but certain.

A silence fell over the group. It was as if time had paused, and the air seemed to hold its breath. Mr. Katz, responded with encouragement, stood up and clapped, a broad smile spreading across his face.

"You are correct," he said, his voice warm with approval. "A gruesome thought, but true. It seems the cat got on the wrong side of the little one, which explains why she was upset and wanted her grandpa in the first place."

The realization hit me like a wave. The cat had been a part of their lives, but it was just another piece in the puzzle of their household. The cat's death, though tragic, was a reflection of the disquiet that existed beneath the surface. It wasn't just the cat—it was the hidden tensions within the family, the unspoken conflicts that no one had dared to address until now.

Mr. Mousa chuckled, his deep voice resonating with humor despite the somber nature of the tale. "Ah, the cat took her dumpling. Now that's a good one," he said, clapping his hands together in a loud gesture that broke the spell of the moment.

The game resumed, the tension lifting slightly, but the questions still lingered. No one spoke much after that, their words few and far between, as if everyone in the room was lost in their own thoughts. The warmth of the evening and the familiar sounds of the game provided a comforting background, but the shadows felt longer now, as if the story had revealed something that couldn't be unseen.

It was Mr. Mousa who won the game, his deep laugh rumbling in the room as he laid down his final piece with a triumphant flourish. "Dominos," he declared loudly, his voice echoing through the room like a triumphant anthem. The other men groaned good-naturedly, though the hint of a smile tugged at the corners of their mouths.

"Well played," my grandfather said, a hint of pride in his voice. "You have the luck of the ancestors today, Mr. Mousa."

Mr. Mousa chuckled and leaned back in his chair, a satisfied look on his face. "Ah, Augustus," he said, shaking his head with a grin, "it's not luck. It's skill and a bit of patience."

My grandfather stood, his back straight and proud, as he gently took my hand in his. "Let's go home, little one," he said, his voice soft but firm.

I nodded, my mind still whirling with the events of the day. I could still feel the weight of his words about children, about life—and death. There was something in my chest that had shifted, something I couldn't explain, but I knew I would carry it with me for a long time.

We walked back home in silence, the fading light casting long shadows on the path. The world felt a little different now, and I wasn't sure if I was ready to face it just yet. My grandfather's voice broke the silence as we approached our front door. He said, little one a name he called me until his last breath, one of my dear friends in that very room was a child soldier at the age of seven. I will check in on him tomorrow as his memories may keep him awake tonight. A soldier as a child! I exclaimed. Yes, children can kill, and will kill whether they are trained to do so or not. He never told me which of his lifelong friends was a child soldier I was left to guess as you all are.

The children were quiet, Cha jr. stated confidently that killing animals was wrong and then he started to cry. Lorna agreed but explained that, it was not a true story it was a made, up mystery story to be solved. At this point the girls started to chant "crybaby". Lorna hushed everyone and promised them a fun story about the largest pumpkin ever.

Chapter 4 — Harvesting

My Grandparents were farmers; among other occupations they held in the village. Each planting season, I was allowed to choose which vegetable I wanted to grow and harvest. This was always an exciting time for me; at the age of eight, the entire process felt magical.

Last spring, I planted corn with my grandpa. His hands, large and weathered from years of hard work, moved with surprising precision as he made small holes in the earth. He had an effortless way of working the land, his brown skin slightly darkened under the sun, and his movements steady as he dug with the same rhythm that had been passed down through generations. I held three small corn kernels in my hand, marveling at their size compared to the vast patch of earth we would soon fill with rows of plants. The rich soil was a mixture of dark brown and black, warm to the touch, as my fingers pressed into it. My grandfather's voice broke the quiet work.

"Three kernels, little one. Three to a hole. That's how the corn will grow."

I smiled up at him, looking into his strong face, shaded by his wife, brimmed hat, and nodded as I gently placed each kernel into the small holes we had made, covering them with the earth until the patch was fully planted. My grandfather worked beside me, his large hands creating a rhythm that I tried to keep up with. It felt like we were part of something much older than either of us—something deep and rooted in the earth.

This year, I chose pumpkins. I remembered how large Kye's pumpkins had grown the previous year, and how everyone praised him for their size. Kye was Mr. Tang's grandson, and the tallest boy in our school. He had broad shoulders and long limbs, his skin sun-kissed from working outside with his grandfather. I watched him from a distance, envious of his confidence and the admiration he seemed to draw from everyone around him. He had a calm, steady way about him, as if he already knew the world, and I couldn't help but feel both drawn to him and slightly resentful. When we were younger, we would sneak off together to play jacks, laughing and forgetting the world around us. But when other boys were around, Kye was different. He acted like I didn't matter, and it hurt more than I wanted to admit.

My grandfather patiently explained that pumpkins needed space for their vines to spread, and that once the vines bloomed, they needed to be left undisturbed. "Don't touch them too much, little one," he cautioned. "The pumpkin's vine must be left alone to grow properly. If you disturb it, the pumpkins won't grow as big as they should."

I took his advice seriously, listening carefully as we chose the perfect spot for the pumpkin patch. It was just outside my bedroom window, a place where I could keep an eye on the plants every day. The soil there was rich, and the patch was far enough from Mr. Mousa's fence that the vines wouldn't be trampled.

In the beginning, nothing much happened. I visited the patch every day, expecting to see a vine pushing through the soil, but for days it remained bare. Finally, the first vine sprouted, small and green, the leaves unfurling slowly like new life stretching to greet the sun. I rushed to show Grandpa, and his proud smile made me even more excited. I watched every day, waiting for the pumpkins to grow. With each day, the vine spread farther, its long tendrils curling around the ground. It was magical to watch something I had planted grow so quickly.

Over time, my pumpkins grew. One vine from my largest pumpkin even stretched through Mr. Mousa's fence and into his yard. I often checked on it, amazed at how large it was growing, even though Kye had little interest in it. He was growing potatoes that year, and when I told him about my pumpkins, he simply shrugged and said, "That's old news," as though my achievement was unimportant compared to his potatoes.

Despite his dismissal, I continued to care for my pumpkins. They grew large and round, their orange skins becoming vibrant under the sun. Each, day I checked them, waiting for the perfect moment to harvest them. My grandfather would always walk with me, inspecting each pumpkin, his voice filled with quiet pride as he encouraged me to wait until they were truly ready.

"Soon," he would say. "The pumpkins are nearly there. You'll have your reward."

On the night of a full moon, when the sky was clear and bright, two of my pumpkin vines detached. The next morning, I rushed to my Grandparents room and jumped on their bed with excitement, waking Grandpa up from sleep. "Harvest time!" I shouted, grinning from ear to ear. "I'm going to be famous! I grew a pumpkin bigger than Kye's, and everyone's going to know!"

Grandma, who was already awake, gave me a gentle but firm look and told me to calm down before I ran off to harvest the pumpkins. The sun was still low in the sky as we set off, and the crisp air smelled of fresh dew. My grandfather carried his machete, a tool he had used for years to harvest crops, and I pushed the wheelbarrow ahead of him. Together, we sang *This Old Man*, my favorite song, as we worked.

We harvested all the pumpkins in our yard and then waited for Mr. Mousa to wake up so we could retrieve the largest one, the pumpkin that had grown beyond all expectations.

When Mr. Mousa finally came out to greet us, he was his usual friendly self. A tall man with a broad frame, he wore a simple shirt and trousers, his dark skin glowing in the early morning light. His smile was warm, and he waved as we approached. Grandpa exchanged a few words with him, and I rushed to the patch. My heart raced with anticipation as I lifted the largest pumpkin into my arms. It was heavier than I expected, but it felt like a triumph to carry it.

Mrs. Mousa joined us soon after. She was a kind woman, shorter than her husband but with a presence that was just as strong. Her skin, a rich dark brown, shone under the sunlight, and her eyes twinkled with warmth. She was always smiling, always moving with grace and purpose. She was the kind of woman who made you feel at ease, who never seemed rushed, and always took the time to listen.

She lifted her camera, capturing the moment as I stood proudly beside my pumpkin. The warm sunlight illuminated the scene, casting a soft glow on the pumpkin and my face, as if highlighting this small victory. Mrs. Mousa smiled as she clicked the shutter, her voice filled with affection. "What a beauty!" she said. "Your hard work paid off, my dear."

"Grandpa!" I called. "Quick, help me get it off the vine!"

My grandfather knelt beside me and carefully detached the pumpkin. Then, still kneeling, he lifted the massive pumpkin into his arms. He beckoned me over and placed my hand on the vegetable, then called for Mr. Mousa.

"My granddaughter," he announced proudly, "is honored to present you with this pumpkin as a token of her gratitude for letting it grow in your yard."

Mr. Mousa smiled warmly and thanked us for the care we had shown. He assured me that the pumpkin had been no trouble at all and that watching it grow by his wife's rose bush had been a joy.

I was devastated. Overcome with emotion, I burst into tears — no, I wailed. I collapsed to the ground, mumbling a flurry of incoherent words, perhaps even a curse or two — I can't quite remember.

Mrs. Mousa, with her ever-present grace, called for my grandmother. Her voice, filled with concern, seemed to cut through the fog of my distress. My grandmother rushed over, her worn hands gently pulling me into her arms, enveloping me in the warmth and safety of her embrace. She hugged me tightly, rocking me gently back and forth, her soft hums soothing me as I struggled to quiet the storm inside.

My grandfather, seeing my anguish, lifted me effortlessly onto his broad shoulder. His hands, strong and steady, held me securely as he carefully began to walk. The strength in his grip reminded me that I was safe, that I was loved, and that I would find peace again. My grandmother followed behind us, her footsteps slow but steady, as she hummed a tune that filled the air with a sense of calm.

We walked in silence, the dirt path beneath our feet soft and worn from years of use. The sounds of the village faded away, replaced by the distant rush of water. Soon, we reached the riverbank, the coolness of the air near the water contrasting with the warmth of the sun on my skin. The river flowed steadily before us, its surface reflecting the blue sky above, the ripples of the water catching the light in delicate patterns.

Grandpa sat down with me still perched on his shoulder. He shifted me into his lap, his strong, familiar hands supporting me as I rested against his chest. He placed his forehead gently against mine, his voice soft but firm as he spoke.

"The ocean and the river never have to ask permission from anyone whose property they pass through, flood, or destroy," he said, his voice steady and wise. "But as people, when we use someone else's space—whether intentionally or not—we should acknowledge it, and if possible, repay their kindness."

His words, simple yet profound, hung in the air like a whisper of truth carried by the wind. The river beside us continued its steady flow, unbothered by the world around it, as though it had always known its path.

He then placed me down gently in his lap, his arms still around me, comforting me as he asked, "Are you a mighty river or an ocean?"

I shook my head softly, my voice barely a whisper. "No."

Grandpa pulled me close again, his embrace tighter now, as if to remind me that no matter the weight of the world or the mistakes we made, love and understanding would always be there to guide me.

By: Olga Foreign   Conversations with My Grandfather

Later that day, my grandmother walked me back to the Mousas' home. The walk was quiet, the warmth of the afternoon sun wrapping around us like a blanket. The soft rustling of the trees was the only sound that accompanied us as I gathered my courage and I delivered the best apology my eight, year, old self could manage.

Agustus, still with a look of disbelief, asked, *"Did you not even get a slice of that pumpkin?"* His voice was tinged with curiosity, as if he couldn't fathom how such a moment could slip away unnoticed. Lorna chuckled softly, remembering the event vividly.

She did, I later enjoyed several pieces, thanks to Mrs. Mousa, who cooked it the way Lorna loved it, boiled pumpkin with butter.

But despite that, Lorna could never forget the way Kye's face had lit up when he first saw the picture of me holding that gigantic pumpkin. His surprise was almost comical, as if he'd discovered an entirely different version of me.

At that moment, the children, eager to contribute to the conversation, began chattering excitedly about their own choices. They started debating who they would be if given the chance—whether a river or an ocean. It was as though the idea of picking something so vast and limitless was far more important than the humble pumpkin we'd just discussed.

"If I could have kept my pumpkin," little Merry declared, her face scrunched in thought, *"I would have said I am a mighty river, and I want my pumpkin."*

The room burst into laughter at the innocence of her statement, and for a fleeting moment, I felt the weight of time shift. I could see that the children were beginning to understand the importance of stories, of choices, of identity—and yet, the playful energy of youth was still very much alive in them.

My father, ever the calming presence, gently interjected, his deep voice cutting through the excitement. *"Alright, children, calm down now. There are still two more stories to go."*

His words brought a moment of stillness, and the chatter slowly faded as the children turned their attention back to me. I took a deep breath, feeling the weight of the moment shift, and with a quiet smile, I turned the page in my book, signaling the beginning of the next story. The room quieted in anticipation, and I began.

Chapter 5 — World Within

My grandfather was deeply in tune with the earth. He seemed to know every beast, insect, tree, bush, weed, bird, and fish—or at least that's how I remember him. The way he moved through the world, his large, calloused hands touching everything with reverence, seemed to connect him to nature in a way that I could never quite understand.

He always refused my requests to join him and my male cousins on their bush walks. To be honest, it wasn't entirely his decision. My grandmother's sharp glance dared him to even consider saying yes. So instead, I spent those days learning to sew, cook, dance, and weave baskets. The smells of the kitchen—the rich, fragrant herbs, the sweet and savory mixes of spices—mingled with the warm, earthy scents of the garden. But no matter how hard I tried, I was convinced the boys were having far more fun. I longed to see the wild places my grandfather spoke of—the dark forests and open fields, where everything seemed to hum with life.

It took me until I was twelve to finally earn a place on one of those bush walks. By then, I was deemed sensible enough, stronger, and—most importantly—had developed what my grandfather called "common sense." Apparently, common sense was an essential tool for a girl in the bush. I always suspected only the girls needed this extra qualification. By that point, my grandmother had also abandoned her attempts to teach me her cooking techniques, so my opportunity arrived without much resistance.

That day, I walked side by side with my grandfather, his long stride matching the rhythm of the earth beneath us. He wore his favorite broad-brimmed straw hat, which shaded his face from the harsh sun. His sturdy, earth, colored trousers, worn thin from years of use, were tucked into leather boots that had been scuffed from countless journeys across rugged terrain. A small, weathered canvas backpack hung loosely from his broad shoulders, filled with supplies—herbs, tools, and a small flask of water—though he carried it more out of habit than necessity. The scent of leather and earth clung to his clothing, and his shirt, a faded checkered flannel, clung to his muscular frame, the sleeves rolled up to his elbows to allow the air to cool him.

My own attire was less practical but made for comfort in the way that only a young girl's clothes could be. I wore a simple cotton dress, faded with use and the sun's rays, the light fabric blowing gently in the breeze. The dress was a pale yellow, dotted with small flowers, though the colors had long since softened from repeated washings. A pair of leather sandals, well-worn and scraped by rough paths, adorned my feet. I had no pack or basket—those would come later, my grandfather said, when I was ready. For now, I simply carried a small bundle of cloth in my hand, tucked inside which was a few bandages, a small knife for safety, and a scrap of paper where I had written notes about the plants and trees we might encounter. The sandals, though comfortable, had thin soles that sometimes pressed painfully against the jagged rocks, and I winced each time I stepped on one. But the discomfort was nothing compared to the thrill of walking in the wild.

Perhaps sensing my thoughts, he glanced down at me and asked, "Tired yet?"

I shook my head and smiled. "I'm grown now, Grandpa."

He chuckled softly, his deep voice rumbling like distant thunder. Then he began asking me to name the trees we passed, his fingers gently brushing the bark of each trunk. This time, though, he didn't just teach me their names—he told me which ones were useful. His hands moved with such purpose as he showed me how to identify the bark, the leaves, the roots—each one a potential remedy or tool. He did the same for the bushes, weeds, and even insects. He explained which insects nested by certain plants and why they chose those spots—how they, too, needed protection.

As we walked, my grandfather collected cuttings from various bushes, trees, and weeds, gathering sap and even insects along the way. The scents of the forest—rich and earthy, tinged with the sweet perfume of blooming wildflowers and the sharp bite of resin—filled the air. He explained each collection in detail—what it would be used for, when it was best to harvest, and why timing mattered. I half listened, more entranced by the rhythm of his words and the song of the forest than the lessons themselves.

He knew I was only pretending to pay attention. My true reason for insisting on joining this bush walk was to witness the honeycomb harvest.

When we stopped for lunch, my grandfather began clapping his hands in a steady rhythm, like a heartbeat. His calloused palms struck together with a soft slap, the sound sharp and purposeful against the stillness of the forest. Then he began to recite a mantra, his voice low and melodic, each word punctuated by the clap of his hands.

- "A tree and a man can sprout new buds.

- Ice and soap carry no germs.

- The poison and the antidote are twelve feet apart.

- The earth and time heal all wounds.

- Water is the strongest force on Earth.

- Everything eats, and everything dies.

- All who shall meet have met before.

- In you is a world."

He had me repeat the mantra over and over, clapping my hands in time with his rhythm. The air seemed to vibrate with each word, each repetition sinking deeper into my mind and heart. After about ten repetitions, I could say it by heart, the words now part of me, echoing in my chest like a pulse.

We continued our walk, the forest now alive with the hum of insects and the rustling of leaves overhead. My grandfather showed me a bush with poisonous berries, their deep purple hue almost inviting. The air was thick with the scent of the ripe fruit; a warning wrapped in beauty. He turned his back, pacing out twelve steps, and called me over. There, he pointed out a plant—the antidote bush.

"This isn't always the case," he warned, his voice gentle but firm, "but if you're in danger, this method might help you find the cure. If not, look for an insect's nest near the poison bush. They often make their home close to the antidote."

The earth beneath our feet seemed to shift with the weight of the knowledge he passed down. Every step was deliberate; every action steeped in generations of wisdom.

Finally, we arrived at the honeycomb tree. My grandfather, ever the patient teacher, prepared a pile of dried tobacco leaves at the base of the tree. The leaves, brown and crisp, crackled softly as he arranged them. "Stay still," he whispered. "Silence is key." His voice, though quiet, held a command that was impossible to ignore.

He fanned the smoke from the tobacco leaves up the tree using large banana leaves, the sweet, earthy scent rising into the air. The smoke curled in the still air, a quiet invitation to the bees. Then, crafting a smoke torch, he lit a cigar, the smell of tobacco mingling with the fresh green scent of the forest. With the ease of someone who had done this countless times, he climbed the tree, his hands moving with the confidence of a man who had made this journey more times than he could count.

My climbing skills were good, but I could never match his confidence and grace. He reached the beehive with ease, puffing on his cigar, and blew smoke across the hive's entrance. He shifted to the other side of the tree and repeated the process several times. Then, moving swiftly, he reached in and carefully pulled out a chunk of honeycomb, the golden honey dripping sweetly onto the bark. My mouth watered as the scent of honey filled the air, thick and rich like sunlight captured in wax.

Moments later, he landed on the ground with a soft thud and handed me the honeycomb, wrapped in a banana leaf. The honey was still warm, and I couldn't wait to taste it. The sweetness filled my mouth, a pure, unfiltered delight.

My grandfather hurriedly covered the tobacco fire with banana leaves and stomped on the ground to extinguish the embers. Then, to my surprise, he uncovered the fire again. "Turn around," he instructed. I heard him urinating on the embers—a final measure to ensure the fire was completely out.

On the walk home, I gnawed eagerly on my honeycomb, savoring its sweetness, the natural nectar melting on my tongue. My grandfather sang an ancient tune about how small we are in the world. I barely paid attention to where I was going—I simply followed his footsteps, content to be in his presence, absorbing the world he had shown me.

When he stopped, I bumped into him. He turned, steadying me, and asked gently, "Did you enjoy your treat?"

"YES!" I grinned; my heart full of joy.

He knelt before me, cupped my face in his large, warm hands, and repeated the final line of the mantra.

"In you is a world. Do you know what that means?" he asked softly.

I thought for a moment, then shook my head, unsure of the depth behind his words. Patiently, he smiled. "Each living thing has its own world, and each living thing carries a world within it. The bees have their world in their hive, and today, you consumed a part of that world. The bees consumed the pollen from flowers—a part of their world. We humans take from all these worlds to sustain ourselves. Remember to say thank you and goodbye to the world you've just consumed."

That day, with honey still sweet on my tongue, I whispered my first "thank you" to the bees—and to the world within them.

The children erupted in shouts of a world within me in unison. Lorna was totally caught off guard. She was not expecting that reaction. They wanted to know what the world within them looked like. Sima one of Lorna's father grandchildren knew with certainty her world was filled with chocolate not honey as she like chocolate the most. Lorna grinned and picked her up as she was sure she was right. Merry, brought out a tray of peanut cookies and jugs of lemonade. The children made a chaotic line with their best manners of please and thank you. As we all remember from our time as a child one shall never miss out on cookie time because you forgot your manners.

Once again Lorna with the help of Agustus got the sugar rushed kids to sit for the next and last story of the day.

By: Olga Foreign   Conversations with My Grandfather

Chapter 6 – Healing with Earth & Time

Once the children hushed. Lorna, once again adjusted her glasses and opened her book. Does everyone know the large sugar cane field up the hill? The children responded with yes. Now the harvest is done with large machines. However, when I was a child, the harvest was done by men after a controlled field burn. The field burn usually occurred a day or two before the harvest.

The sugar cane harvest was known for its dangers, and my grandfather always prepared well in advance for a field burn. This season's burn had already claimed two lives. In emergencies, burn victims were often brought to my grandfather's back porch for help.

That season, I was fifteen years old. My body had changed—not to my liking—but somehow my Grandparents seemed incredibly pleased with their DNA's accomplishment. Compliments about my height, beauty, and intelligence were constant and embarrassing. I was old enough now to pay attention to the world beyond my immediate family and friends, and I often found myself observing the people around me more closely. The world outside seemed to be unfolding in a way that was both thrilling and confusing.

On the day it happened, I stood on the porch as I witnessed burnt bodies being brought in—their charred skin a stark reminder of the harvest's risks. The heat of the day was oppressive, and the air around us felt thick with smoke. The scent of burning sugarcane hung heavily in the air, mingling with the sharp tang of ash that clung to everything. My heart beat in my chest as I watched the men carry the burn victims to my grandfather's back porch. Their bodies were blackened, and their faces were beyond recognition. The men, though careful, moved quickly, their footsteps echoing on the worn wooden planks.

With all the knowledge my Grandparents had patiently taught me over the years, I jumped in to help. My hands were shaking, but my mind was clear. I moved as fast as I could, working with the practiced urgency I had learned from watching them. I didn't hesitate when it came to grabbing towels and cloths to wipe the sweat from the victims' faces. The skin on my own hands stung from the heat and the pressure of what was happening around me.

Then they brought him in. His body was completely burned, and most of his hair was gone. His skin was darkened, almost unrecognizable. My grandmother immediately knelt beside him, her movements fluid, practiced. She tilted his head back, listening closely for breath. "Watch his chest," she instructed me, her voice calm yet sharp. "Tell me if you see movement."

I stared hard at his chest, willing myself to see the faintest rise and fall. The air was thick with tension, and the silence around us was so complete

I could hear the slight rustling of the leaves outside, the faint crackle of embers in the distance. My grandmother, satisfied that life still clung to him, shouted for a pit to be dug.

I ran to fit the hose onto the backyard water spigot, the water rushing from the nozzle in powerful jets as I dragged the hose toward the men who were already digging the pit. The earth beneath my feet was soft, damp from the recent rains, and the scent of the soil was rich and grounding. The women worked quickly alongside the men, assisting anyone they could. Some burn victims had been sent to the hospital, but many refused to go, trusting only my Grandparents' traditional medicine over Western practices.

Once the pit was completed, my grandfather began adding herbs and ointments—what seemed like the entire contents of the forest—into the pit. The smell of crushed leaves, earth, and herbs filled the air, mingling with the sharp scent of the fire that still lingered in the surroundings. He added water, yeast, and mixed the concoction until the pit was filled with a thick, muddy herbal blend. It was pungent, thick with earthy tones that made my stomach twist, but I kept my focus on the task at hand.

The burned man was kept unconscious by my grandmother. Bamboo tubes were placed in his nostrils for air, and his ears, mouth, and other openings were sealed with beeswax. The quiet murmurs of the women around us seemed to blend with the rhythmic sounds of digging and preparation. The sun, now low in the sky, bathed the backyard in a warm, golden light, casting long shadows across the yard as the preparations continued.

Then, they carefully lowered his body into the pit, angling him at 45 degrees, his head resting against the ground for support. My grandmother reached into the pit, her hands steady and gentle as she carefully packed the cool herbal mud over his head and face, layer upon layer. Her movements were slow, deliberate, every action filled with a deep sense of care. Periodically, she would check for breath, her hands resting softly on his chest, her eyes narrowing in concentration as she felt for even the faintest movement.

"He's surfacing," she announced, her voice calm but filled with a quiet sense of relief. "He's going to need help when his mind and body become aware again."

My father, rarely seen at my grandfather's home, quietly began gathering the men. "Bring the drums," he ordered, his voice low but firm. "Hurry— we must save Oscar."

It wasn't until I heard that name that I felt the air leave my lungs. Oscar. My first love, the boy four years older than me. The one I'd secretly admired for two years. The one I'd imagined myself marrying one day. The weight of those memories, suddenly overwhelming, made my chest tighten.

It seemed the entire village had heard the call, and soon they descended upon my Grandparents' backyard. The men formed a circle around the pit; their drums tucked between their thighs. The women lit fires, the flickering orange light casting long shadows as they moved about the yard, preparing for the ritual. The rhythmic chanting began—deep and steady, vibrating through the air and the ground beneath us. The sound of the drums was like a heartbeat, resonating in the bones, stirring something deep within.

My grandmother knelt in front of Oscar's mother, cradling her face firmly in her hands. "Repeat after me," she commanded.

"You are Oscar. You are alive. Do not move. Breathe with me. In… one, two, three, four, five… out… one, two, three, four, five… in… one, two, three, four, five… out… one, two, three, four, five… Mom is here. I will never leave you. Repeat it again."

Oscar's mother tried to speak but kept turning her head, desperate to see her son. My grandmother slapped her—hard. The sharp crack echoed across the yard. "Repeat after me!" she demanded.

Finally, Oscar's mother spoke the words with conviction.

My grandmother guided her to Oscar's head, leaned close to his ear, and instructed her, "Speak and do not stop."

The drumbeat continued—steady, powerful, ancient. The chants that followed were not words spoken in everyday language—they were older than memory itself, sounds that resonated in the bones and stirred something deep within. Even the animals stayed still, listening in quiet respect.

My grandmother checked Oscar's breathing again. This time, she locked eyes with his mother—a silent challenge, daring her not to falter.

"Don't stop," she whispered.

And she didn't. Oscar's mother kept speaking, kept chanting, kept breathing in rhythm with her son—her voice steady and strong.

The drumbeat thumped on, pulsing like a heartbeat in the air—and somewhere, beneath layers of healing earth and mud, I knew Oscar was fighting to find his way home

The muddy concoction was always kept moist. The men took turns with the chanting and drumming, while Oscar's grandmother, aunts, and sister took shifts whispering in his ear and breathing with him. I ran as many errands as I could, helping wherever needed, all the while stealing anxious glances at Oscar.

The air around us seemed charged with energy, the chanting echoing in the trees, and the rhythmic thumping of the drums reverberated deep within my chest. The heat of the day hung heavy, the sun burning high in the sky, its rays slicing through the leaves of the trees above us. The scent of burning wood and herbs mixed with the earthiness of the soil, as though everything in the world had gathered in this one place for this one purpose.

On the third day, my grandfather began the delicate process of removing the mud from Oscar's face and head. The mud was thick and caked, clinging to his skin in dried layers. My grandfather worked slowly, his hands gentle but sure, moving with the precision of someone who had done this many times before. His fingers brushed delicately over Oscar's skin as he dried the mud, encouraging it to flake off in small, careful pieces.

The smell of fresh whey filled the air as my grandfather used it to clean the surface of Oscar's skin. The whey, slightly sour, was the perfect antidote to the sticky remnants of the herbal mud. I watched, awestruck, as my grandfather's skilled hands restored Oscar's face, slowly uncovering the features I had longed to see. His once, raw skin began to soften, the blackened patches giving way to the warm, sun-kissed hue I remembered from before. The transformation was nothing short of miraculous.

Once Oscar's face was clean, my grandfather replaced the dried mud with a fresh mixture of aloe, ginger, snail extract, and honey. The sweet scent of honey wafted through the air as he carefully smoothed the soothing paste across Oscar's skin. The honey, golden and thick, clung to his skin like a second layer, the warmth of it offering a strange sense of comfort.

Fresh elephant ear leaves were then placed over the mixture, their large, broad surfaces acting as a protective barrier. The green of the leaves contrasted against the rich honey, colored paste on Oscar's face, making the scene look both beautiful and surreal.

Finally, my grandfather removed the wax seal from Oscar's mouth, hoping his lungs and throat had begun to heal. As he did, Oscar's lips trembled, and with a weak exhale, he breathed through his mouth for the first time in days. It was a shallow, hesitant breath, but it was enough. My grandfather let out a relieved sigh, a sound that seemed to lift the weight from the air around us.

"He's breathing through his mouth," my grandfather murmured, more to himself than anyone else. It was a hopeful sign, but I could see the caution in his eyes—hope, tempered by years of experience and knowledge.

My grandmother then stepped forward and declared, "The men's chanting may end, and the women's chanting may now begin."

The change in rhythm was palpable. The men stopped their drumming, and the women, with their softer, higher voices, began to sing in a gentle, lilting tone. The songs they sang were filled with hope, with faith, and with an ancient rhythm that seemed to resonate in the very air itself. It was a song of healing, of bringing the spirit back to life, of calling the lost soul to return.

That night would be Oscar's final one in the pit. The women's voices would be the last strength he would need to face whatever awaited him when he emerged.

As the women gathered in a circle around Oscar, his mother suddenly rushed over to a young woman, embracing her tightly. The sound of her sobs was muffled by the rhythmic chanting, but the desperation in her voice was unmistakable. "You came… just in time," she whispered, her voice breaking. "He needs to hear your voice. Let me teach you what to say."

Curious, I turned to my grandmother and asked, "Who is she?"

"She's Oscar's fiancée," my grandmother replied softly.

The weight of those words settled in my chest. Until that moment, I had clung to the fragile hope that Oscar—my first love, my secret crush—might one day see me the way I had seen him for the past two years. But now I understood. His heart had already belonged to someone else—someone whose voice, in that critical moment, might just be the one to call him back to life.

The women chanted through the night—songs of journey, light, hope, and faith. I stayed close to my grandmother, helping her cook while trying to learn the words to the songs the women sang. This was my first time taking part in a ritual that seemed instinctual to the village adults. I had grown up hearing the stories, but now I was finally a part of the healing.

I set aside my broken heart and immersed myself in learning as much as I could about this world that was now being revealed to me. The women's voices were steady and filled with power, each note carrying the weight of the past and the future, binding them to the earth, to each other, and to Oscar.

Oscar slept soundly through the night, nourished with warm broth and water at regular intervals. As dawn broke, the women brought their chanting to a close with a long, sustained hum—low and steady, like the earth itself exhaling. The world seemed to breathe with them.

On cue, water was poured into the pit. Two men climbed in and began stomping the mud, their feet moving rhythmically as though they were treading grapes. The sound of their movements, the splashes of water, and the deep thudding of their feet in the mud created a soundscape that was both foreign and deeply familiar. My grandfather stood at the edge, giving instructions with quiet authority, his steady presence grounding everyone around him.

I watched in awe. How did they know to do this? Where was it written? Who had passed down this knowledge? My mind buzzed with questions, but no one paused to explain—they simply knew. The healing rituals, the chants, the rhythm of the movements—all of it was passed down in the most ancient ways, from generation to generation, like an unbroken thread.

A tub of warm whey awaited Oscar. His entire body was immersed, and my grandfather patiently washed him while my grandmother stood nearby, recording notes as he dictated.

"He'll have some scarring where the burns were most severe," my grandfather said, his voice calm and sure. "But most of his wounds are healing well."

I stared in disbelief. Oscar barely resembled the man who had been lowered into the pit days earlier. His skin, though still fragile, had mended in ways I couldn't have imagined. I was overwhelmed with admiration—once again, I had witnessed my Grandparents' quiet magic.

Unable to hold back, I rushed to my grandfather and hugged him tightly. I kissed both of his hands, then turned to my grandmother, cupping her face and pressing a kiss to her cheek.

My grandfather smiled down at me. "Earth and time heal all wounds, little one," he said softly. Then, as if reading my heart, he added, "And time will heal yours, just as the earth healed his." I swallowed hard. It seemed they had always known how I felt about Oscar. And somehow, I knew that time would heal me, just as it had healed him.

The children were silent for a long moment with disbelief. They couldn't understand how being buried in a pit could save someone. Lorna's father spoke up at that moment. It's all true. I was there. I witness it. The Earth has unique healing properties that we are still discovering. Our ancestors knew These ways and they passed them down. Now, that you have heard your three stories for today, follow me. We're going out to the field and the men are going to teach you all how to play the drums and how to chant to save a life. let's go children.

CHAPTER 7, No Family Secret

The final day of the weekend is bittersweet as the family prepares to return to their homes. The children have been soaking in Lorna's stories, and now there's a quiet understanding among them that these tales are part of their heritage, their shared legacy. They were playing in the backyard, making the most of their last afternoon before the long journey back.

Lorna went to them and gathered the children one last time under the cotton tree, ready to share her final stories, tales that will leave them with a deeper understanding of family, love, and responsibility. This weekend we are here celebrating Agustus graduation From College. This next story is about my graduation from high school weekend. You will recognize a good deal of the family ritual we did this weekend and realize just how long this family has been doing the same greetings, meal preparations and demonstrating love for each other.

The sun was in its one o'clock position, casting a warm glow over the family. As Lorna reflects on the stories she's told, she realizes that this weekend isn't just about sharing memories—it's about passing on the lessons of their ancestors. She looks at Agustus, who now has a newfound respect for the stories, and she realizes that this kind of storytelling had strengthened the bonds that will keep the family connected, no matter the distance. Lorna adjusts her glasses and opened her book to the first page. They, may have found it strange that she was now reading the first story in her journal however, no one mentioned that peculiar fact. With a loud and clear voice Lorna began her story.

My graduation was just a day away. I was finally qualified to leave high school, and the whole family had descended on my Grandparents' home, following the long-standing family tradition. The lineage lineup had begun, a ritual passed down for generations. It was a way to honor our elders and recognize the strength of family ties.

The eldest son, my Uncle Marley, arrived first with his family. Marley was a large man with broad shoulders and a commanding presence, but his deep, set eyes carried warmth, making him approachable despite his size. His weathered face spoke of years spent working the land, and his thick, calloused hands were a testament to his hard work. Grandpa stepped forward, placing his forehead against Uncle Marley's in the traditional greeting. They held the connection for a moment, then pulled back to look each other in the eye before hugging—heart to heart, as was our custom. Marley's wife, Josephine, followed the same pattern, greeting Grandpa and then Grandma in the same reverent way. Josephine was a striking woman, tall with dark, glowing skin and smooth, silver hair pulled into a neat bun. Her presence was calm and regal, and her smile had the warmth of a thousand sunrises. Their children, Sha, Cha, and Yuha, followed, each pressing foreheads and matching heartbeats as they hugged. Sha was the eldest and already stood tall like her father, her thick braids cascading down her back. Cha, quieter and more reserved, had an elegant air about her, and little Yuha, with his wide, inquisitive eyes, was always the playful one, always the first to ask a thousand questions.

Next in line was my Uncle Joseph, accompanied by his wife Mary and their only daughter, Merry. Uncle Joseph had a quieter demeanor. His dark hair, speckled with graying strands, and his thoughtful eyes gave him an air of quiet authority. His skin, though not as weathered as Marley's, still carried the marks of years spent in labor. His wife, Mary, was soft-spoken and gentle, always with a kind word for everyone. Merry, their daughter, was a lively girl of about my age, with a mischievous sparkle in her eye. She was full of energy and always wore a smile that lit up the room. Uncle Joseph greeted Grandpa by touching foreheads, then embraced him heart to heart. This pattern continued as Uncle Map and Uncle Euless greeted the elders. Uncle Euless, who remained unmarried, approached alone but was greeted with the same respect. Uncle Map, or as I usually called him—Dad, arrived with his wife and their two sons, Anthony and Map Jr. Each followed the tradition, greeting Grandpa and Grandma with forehead touches and heart-to-heart hugs.

Once all the adults had greeted each other, the children followed, pressing their foreheads together and then sharing a heart, hug. Laughter and warmth filled the air as cousins reunited, exchanging stories of school and life. The feeling of connection was palpable, and I couldn't help but feel a profound sense of pride. This wasn't just about my graduation—it was about the unbroken chain of family that stretched back through the generations, a legacy woven together by shared memories and traditions. The home seemed to pulse with love, and I felt deeply grateful to be a part of it.

Finally, everyone gathered in the Great Hall for refreshments, the room buzzing with joy and anticipation of the graduation the next day. The Hall was large, with thick wooden beams and large windows that allowed the evening light to flood the room. The stone fireplace crackled in the corner, casting a soft glow that mingled with the laughter and the clinking of glasses. The smell of fresh fruit, sweet pastries, and spices wafted through the room, adding to the festive atmosphere.

As I sat with my cousins, I couldn't help but feel a sense of pride and gratitude. It wasn't just about graduating—it was about the legacy I was part of, one filled with love, respect, and the traditions that kept us connected.

As was customary, the women soon separated and moved into the kitchen, while the men gathered outside under the large cotton tree. The cotton tree, a sentinel in the yard, was a place of history and stories, its thick branches providing shade and shelter from the scorching sun. The tree's leaves rustled gently in the breeze; its deep green foliage alive with life. The children spread out into the backyard, playing and comparing notes on their summer vacations and school sessions. In the kitchen, the women gossiped, caught up on family news, and talked about their children and husbands while preparing the ingredients for lunch and dinner. Yams were washed, corn was shucked, rice was rinsed, and meat was seasoned. The kitchen was alive with laughter and chatter, filled with stories that hadn't been shared since the last gathering.

Under the cotton tree, the men played dominoes, sang, laughed, and talked about their families, work, and the children's accomplishments. They shared their pride and their hopes for the coming year, while the children enjoyed the great weather, playing with the animals, exploring the fields, and wandering through the farm. The golden sunlight filtered through the branches of the tree, casting dappled shadows on the ground where the men sat in a loose circle. The smell of tobacco, mixed with the earthy scent of the soil, made the scene feel timeless, like a ritual that had been carried out for generations.

After about two hours, the men and women switched places. The men took over in the kitchen, using the prepped ingredients to start cooking the lunch meal, while the women gathered under the cotton tree. There, they danced, wove baskets, sang, and shared stories about their dreams, hopes for the future, and the next generation's progress. They spoke of grandchildren, of new skills learned, and of who they were most proud of.

Grandma called the children to take turns washing up and preparing for lunch. We helped set the big backyard table, laying out knives, forks, plates, spoons, and serving utensils as Grandma directed. The air was filled with the scent of warm bread, roasting meats, and freshly prepared vegetables. Once everything was ready, the men served the lunch meal while keeping the fires low on the dinner meal, allowing the food to cook slowly. The entire family came together in the backyard for a joyful, noisy, and memorable lunch, filled with laughter, music, and the happiness of being together.

After the meal, the men returned to the kitchen, playing games and exchanging jokes as they waited for the dinner to be cooked. The women gathered in the Great Hall, bringing the children along. Each woman took turns teaching a skill—knitting, weaving, writing, or reading—to a child who wasn't their own, passing down knowledge and traditions to the next generation.

Meanwhile, my Grandparents sat on the front porch in their rocking chairs, listening to the vibrant sounds of the house filled with family. After a while, they stood up, held hands, and started to take a walk. Curious, I decided to follow them, still adjusting to the sheer number of people around. I wasn't used to it—I was accustomed to just the three of us: Grandma, Grandpa, and me. My dad visited, but I never lived with him, his wife, or his two sons. I never questioned it; Grandpa loved and respected my dad, so I did too.

I followed them at a distance as they moved off the main path toward the family graveyard, a place I seldom visited. There were eight tombstones, including two belonging to my Grandparents' children. I realized they must be feeling a sense of loss, especially with so much family gathered. As they approached the graves, Grandpa gently spoke, "Esther, your daughter is graduating high school. We've done our best by her. I've taught her everything I know. Didn't I, dear?" He looked at Grandma, who nodded, tears streaming down her face. "We did our best. She's a beautiful, smart, kind woman. You'd be proud, my dearest daughter. You'd be proud."

A wave of confusion hit me. Esther—my mother? Until that moment, I hadn't known that my mother was their daughter. I had never asked, never wondered where my mom was. My Grandparents had always been enough. I suddenly realized that my dad wasn't Grandpa's son but his son-in-law. My heart raced with the weight of this revelation.

I couldn't hold back a strangled cry. My Grandparents turned, startled to see me standing there. Grandpa hurried to me, his strong hands gently resting on my shoulders. "Baby girl, what's wrong? What happened?" he asked, his voice filled with concern. I couldn't find the words, overwhelmed by the truth and the memories swirling in my head.

I looked at him, my heart pounding. "Why didn't you tell me?" I whispered. "Why didn't you ever tell me that my mom was your daughter?"

Grandpa looked to Agnus, then said in a determined voice we thought you knew; his eyes were misty. "We wanted you to grow up with love, not loss. You were our little girl's child. We thought it was better this way. Your dad never objected—he knew you were safe and loved here."

Grandma continued, her voice softening. "Your mom was 32 when she passed away from a traffic accident. You were only 4. She was on her way to pick you up from our house when tragedy struck. You cried every day, asking for your mom. Do you not remember? We used to walk with you to this gravesite, place flowers on your mom's grave, and help you talk to her. Around the age of 8, you stopped wanting to visit. You chose life and love instead of loss. We were proud of you, but we never intended to hide this from you."

Grandpa added, "Your father lives in another parish but visits whenever he can. He never wanted his wife to take on the role of your stepmother. He wanted your mom's memory to stay intact, never wanting you to feel like her love was being replaced. "They were deeply in love from the moment they met at medical school. He was broken after her death and not in a good emotional state to be with you.

Grandma placed her hand on my shoulder. "We love your father. He was a good husband to our daughter and a good father to you. We thought you understood, but if you have questions, we're here to answer them."

I looked down at the gravestone, my heart aching but grateful. "I just... never knew," I whispered. Grandpa pulled me into a gentle hug. "We're here, baby girl. Always."

After wiping each other's tears away, we returned to the house. Grandpa, Grandma, and I entered the Great Hall, and Grandpa called for everyone to gather. Once the room was quiet, Grandpa spoke, his voice strong but tender. "Tomorrow morning, before the graduation ceremony, we'd like to invite everyone to take a walk with us to the family cemetery. It's important that we remember those who came before us and honor their memory."

Everyone agreed, and the next morning, the entire family walked together to the cemetery. They crowded around the gravestones, paying their respects, placing flowers, and cleaning off some of the older markers. When we reached Esther's grave, Grandpa spoke softly, sharing stories about her life, her kindness, and her love for me. One by one, family members shared memories, and I felt the weight of love and loss blend into a bittersweet peace. Afterward, we all returned to the house, the somber mood gradually giving way to lighthearted laughter, especially from the children who resumed their games.

Everyone gathered to prepare for the graduation ceremony. As I stood in front of the mirror, adjusting the cream, colored dress Grandma had helped me pick out for the occasion, I couldn't help but feel a rush of emotions. The dress, simple yet elegant, reached just above my knees, its light fabric flowing as I moved. The fabric shimmered softly in the light, and it had delicate lace trim around the neckline. I had braided my hair into an intricate pattern, with small strands of gold beads woven into the braids, giving it a touch of elegance.

Grandma had given me a pair of simple pearl earrings to wear for the occasion. They had belonged to her mother, and every time I wore them, I felt her love and wisdom surrounding me. The pearls sparkled softly against my tanned skin, complementing my simple yet graceful appearance.

Before we left for the school grounds, the elders gathered around me. Each of them had a gift for me, a tradition that marked our family's love and respect. The Great Hall was filled with a quiet hum of anticipation as the family watched this special moment.

Uncle Marley, always the first to speak, came forward, his hands warm as he pressed a small gold bracelet into my palm. It was simple, with delicate engravings along the edges. "Lorna, my dear," he said, his voice steady but filled with emotion. "This is for you, to remind you that you are always a link in this family's chain of strength. Wear it with pride."

I felt a tear well in my eye as I held the bracelet, the weight of his words sinking in. I had never felt more loved, more connected to my family than I did in that moment.

Next, Aunt Josephine stepped forward, her graceful hands holding a small pouch of dried lavender. She smiled warmly at me, her dark eyes gleaming. "Lorna, this is for calmness, for peace," she said softly. "May you always find peace in yourself, just as you bring peace to everyone around you." She kissed my forehead and placed the pouch into my hands. The calming scent of lavender filled the air as she did so, grounding me in the present.

Uncle Joseph, the quiet one, handed me a fine leather-bound journal. "Lorna," he said quietly, his eyes thoughtful, "may this journal be a place for your dreams, your ideas, and your thoughts. Write down your heart, and know that your words carry weight in this world."

I held the journal close, the feel of the soft leather warming my hands. I had always loved writing, but now, with Uncle Joseph's words, I felt a deep sense of purpose, as if my thoughts could shape the world around me.

Uncle Euless, who had always been a bit of an enigma to me, stood with a simple wooden carving of a bird. It was beautifully crafted; each feather perfectly etched into the wood. "Lorna, fly high," he said, his voice quiet but strong. "Never let the world keep you grounded. The sky is your limit."

His words made my heart swell with emotion. The bird, with its outstretched wings, now symbolized something greater to me—freedom, hope, and the endless possibilities that awaited me.

Uncle Map, or "Dad" as I always called him, walked forward with a silver ring. It was elegant but not too flashy, just like him. The ring glinted in the light, and I recognized it as the one he had worn for years on his pinky finger. As he placed it in my hand, I could see his eyes shimmer with emotion.

"Lorna," he said softly, his voice barely above a whisper. "This is your mother's wedding ring. I want you to have it. Your mother was my first love, and you carry so much of her with you. This ring isn't just a symbol of marriage—it's a reminder of the love that built this family, and the strength that flows through you."

I held the ring in my palm, feeling the cold metal warm against my skin. It felt heavy, not just with its physical weight, but with the memories it held. It was as though I could feel my mother's presence through it, and the absence that had shaped so much of my life.

As my hand closed around the ring, my thoughts suddenly drifted to my father, who had always been a distant figure in my life. He had never lived with us since Mom passed away, and yet he had always been careful, loving, and respectful. We never spoke of the void left by my mother, and although I never resented him for it, I didn't fully know him. His visits were few, and each time, he seemed like a stranger—someone who loved me, but with a distance I couldn't understand.

This gift, the ring, was the closest he had ever come to telling me how much my mother had meant to him. I wondered if he had ever felt the weight of her absence as I did. I couldn't hold back the feeling of confusion in my chest, but I didn't feel resentment. It was more like a gap—an unasked question that remained unanswered, and now, as I looked at him, I realized how much I still didn't understand about him.

My father, standing there in his carefully pressed shirt, looked at me with sadness and pride. His eyes, usually so composed, now flickered with something deeper—pain, joy, and perhaps something else I couldn't quite place. As he gazed at me, I wondered if he could see my mother's face in mine, the same soft curve of her cheek, the same shade of brown in her eyes. I realized then that for all the love he had for me, he must have seen his first love in me, his young daughter.

I wondered if he had spent all these years wrestling with the ghost of my mother, trying to be a father without the presence of the woman he had loved so fiercely. It must have been confusing for him—joyful to see me grow, but painful to see the reminder of the love he lost.

Before the family woke up that morning, my father had walked alone to Esther's grave. In the quiet dawn, he had stood there, looking down at the stone that marked his wife's resting place. With tears in his eyes, he had spoken to her in whispers, telling her how proud he was of me, how much I had become the woman they had dreamed of. He had asked for her guidance, he admitted feeling the weight of her absence every day, but also to finally allowing himself to feel not just the loss, but the love that still bound him to her memory. He did not notice me as I had climbed a tree earlier, by my mother's grave, to have my own private talk with her before graduating.

I looked at him now, still holding the ring, and saw the quiet conflict in his eyes. "Dad, I don't know what to say," I whispered, unable to hide the emotions that were welling up in me.

"You don't need to say anything, Lorna," he replied, his voice rough with emotion. "I only wanted you to have this, so you know you were loved by both of us—your mother and me. She's always with you, and I'll always be here too."

His words brought a rush of emotions, and for the first time, I truly felt the depth of his love—silent but steadfast. As I looked into his eyes, I knew I had the space to ask whatever questions I needed, even if I wasn't quite ready yet. And for the first time, I understood that he had always done what was best for me—even when I couldn't understand why he acted the way he did.

The family lined up, and we made our way to the school grounds. The ceremony was beautiful, filled with proud speeches, cheers, and the beaming faces of families watching their graduates' step into the next chapter of their lives. When my name was called, I walked up to the stage, scanning the crowd to see my family clapping, cheering, and waving. It felt like the entire village was there, celebrating together. I felt an overwhelming sense of love and belonging as I crossed the stage, realizing that this moment marked my transition from childhood to adulthood.

Upon returning home, preparations for dinner began with the same lively spirit. Even the children helped Grandma bake pies in the earth oven. Dinner was served with the same warmth and joy, the children setting the table just as before and helping with the cleanup afterward. Grandpa sang in his deep, melodic voice, and the women joined in. We gathered around the fireplace, roasting corn and cashews, making jokes, and sharing stories. I was so excited and filled with love.

As I sat beside Grandpa, he placed his hands on my cheeks, looking me in the eye. "Baby girl," he said softly, "there's really no such thing as a family secret—it's usually just a question unasked. Sometimes we think things are hidden when, in truth, we just never asked to know."

In that moment, I understood. I hadn't asked about my mother, not because I didn't care, but because I had always felt safe and loved. Grandpa wasn't blaming me; he was just reminding me that sometimes, the things we don't know are simply the things we never seek to ask or understand.

Augusta spoke up first once the story was concluded. Mom, I want to know more about Grandma Ester, do you remember her face? What stories do you have about her? I shook my head sadly and replied, my childhood that I remember, were full of my grandmother's and grandfather's face, touch, and smell. I can share with you later Augustus what my Grandparents taught me about my mother and what my father also told me about my mother. Augustus replied, 'thank you mom'. He understood that his not knowing about his grandmother was because he did not ask, it was no secret. I took out an old photograph of my mother and passed it to the children. As they passed it around, Lorna listened to the murmurs of the children's voices saying "she looks like her", or "wow she was beautiful." Lorna smiled knowing that Ester will be remembered. Augustus silently placed the photograph in his wallet; Lorna did not attempt to take it back she felt that picture had found its rightful owner.

Children, Lorna said in a loud but calm voice, you have been wonderful during story time. The next three stories I have to share with you Are all secrets that no one else in the family knows. After today I'm counting on you all to share these three stories with the rest of your family. Can I count on you to listen, and remember. You must retell the stories exactly like I tell them now. The children all responded in their noisy chaotic flavor with yes, nods even some proclaiming they were the best story tellers. Lorna laughed, adjusted her glasses and opened her book, the journal she had received on her high school graduation day.

By: Olga Foreign

Conversations with My Grandfather

Chapter 8 – Appreciation of Life

Lorna began the story by asking a question: "We all know how great my grandmother's sweet potato pudding was, but did you know that she didn't eat chicken? *Yet, she was known throughout our community for making the best stewed chicken. People would line up outside her back kitchen window just to get the gravy, with some dumpling. They didn't even need a piece of chicken—that's how famous my grandmother's stewed brown chicken was.*"

Most of the children shook their heads. Some of the older children had only small memories of my grandmother in her later days, when she no longer cooked as much. Lorna smiled softly, remembering the woman who had nurtured her for so many years. "This story," she continued, "is about the last feast my grandmother ever cooked for me and my grandfather."

It was a day like any other regular day, but it wasn't. I remember it clearly, and always will. My Grandmother was 84 years old, our birthdays were only two days apart, and we celebrated together, as we sometimes did. At that time, I was 32—exactly the same age my mother had been when she died. Grandma married Grandpa Agustus when she was 23, and he was 26. A year after their wedding, they had my mother, Esther. As you know, Esther passed away when she was 32, leaving me under the care of my Grandparents, who were both in their fifties at the time.

Yes, I was 32, and I was living with my Grandparents in my favorite house with my two favorite people. The longest I had spent away from them was during my years at college. Four years living on campus, experiencing severe homesickness. I missed everything: my grandmother's food, the forest, how my Grandparents smelled, their laughter, and the big cotton tree we're sitting under right now. As soon as I could after graduation, I moved right back in, and I've never left. I found a job as an emergency nurse at our local hospital, taking care of the locals just as I saw my Grandparents do as I grew up. Now, I'm getting ready to retire and spend more time with you beautiful children, as much as I can.

As I said, this was a regular day. I woke up, greeted my Grandparents, and helped make breakfast. Our roles had changed somewhat—I seemed to be doing most of the chores now, but my Grandparents still helped and gave guidance where they could. After breakfast, we sat under the cotton tree, all three of us, listening to some of my Grandparents' old songs on the radio.

After a few hours, I prepared lunch. It was a Saturday, and we followed our usual routine: talking about the chores that needed to be done before Monday and the order in which they should be completed, depending on who was available, how long each task would take, and what materials we had.

My grandfather helped me clear the table, while my grandmother went to the bathroom. As I stood in front of the kitchen sink, preparing to wash the dishes, my grandfather spoke softly.

"Lorna, your grandmother doesn't want you to know, but she hasn't been feeling well. The doctor gave her some medication, but she doesn't want to take it. Could you talk to her for me?" he asked, his voice laced with concern.

I rinsed my hands in the sink and turned to him. *"What's the medication for? Why didn't I know about this? When did she go to the doctor?"*

My grandfather held up his hand, signaling me to slow down. *"She went last week, while you were visiting your father. I think it's serious. Sometimes, she coughs up blood. But she says the doctor said it's not serious, that she just needs to take her medication when she feels it's necessary. She's never kept anything from me, but this time... I can tell she doesn't want to share her condition with me. I'm not sure why. Could you please speak with her?"*

I nodded, rinsed my hands off, and immediately went to find my grandmother. I tried to calm myself; as usual, anything that could be negative regarding my Grandparents made me anxious. My grandmother had returned to the dining room, sitting at the table while my grandfather stayed in the kitchen, washing dishes.

I sat beside her and gently took her hand. *"Grandma, tell me about your doctor's visit. How were you feeling before you went? What did the doctor say?"*

Grandma tilted her head to the right and glanced toward the kitchen, as if catching a glimpse of Grandpa. Then she looked at me directly and said, *"Did he ask you to come talk to me?"*

I nodded. *"Yes."*

"Should I be worried?" I asked. Grandma gently patted my hands and replied, *"Lorna, we're both old. Your grandfather and I have seen a lot. We've eaten a lot. We've laughed a lot. We've enjoyed life. We will get sick, and when it's our time, it's our time. Just like with Wishes our donkey, do you remember?"*

At this point, I gripped her hand tightly. *"Grandma, are you alright?"* I asked, feeling an overwhelming rush of worry.

She reached out and cupped my faced in both her hands, the same way both she and Grandpa always did when they were about to tell me something important and wanted my full attention.

My grandmother then spoke in a soft voice. *"Sometimes, I can't seem to catch my breath. My chest hurts, and when I cough, sometimes there's blood. So, I went to see the doctor. He ran some tests, but I haven't received the results yet. He gave me some medicine for when the pain gets too bad. Your grandfather thinks I'm holding something back from him, but I'm not. I truly don't know what's wrong with me. I won't know until I return to the doctor next Thursday. He mentioned that it could be cancer, a virus, or just aging. I didn't share all those possibilities with your grandfather because possibilities are just that—possibilities. When I know, we all will know."*

I took a deep breath, understanding the seriousness of the situation. *"I understand, Grandma. I'll take the day off work and go with you. We all will know."*

She nodded. *"Don't tell your grandfather the possibilities. He'll only worry. Just tell him, like I told you—that I don't know, but I'll know more on Thursday. And let him know that you'll be there with me, and he doesn't need to come. Though I'm sure he'll try. Just tell him you'll go with me, alright?"*

I stood up and hugged my grandmother tightly. Then I walked to the kitchen to speak with my grandfather, repeating the information as my grandmother had wished. We continued through the weekend, all three of us trying to hide our feelings and emotions from each other, not wanting to cause any more worry. Thursday seemed so Far away.

My grandfather kept himself busy, brewing every remedy he knew to help my grandmother with her pain and shortness of breath. He was certain it was just a case of pneumonia and that she needed to rest, so he sought every opportunity to make sure she sat down.

The next day, Sunday, the house was eerily quiet. I woke up, and as I usually did, I went to my Grandparents' room. They typically rose earlier than I did, and I was used to hearing their soft voices chatting in the living room. But this morning, there was almost no sound at all. My Grandparents were still in bed. Grandpa was snuggled closely to Grandma. He opened his eyes and, seeing me, said softly, "We'll be with you soon, dear child. We'll be with you soon. Go fix breakfast now. We're getting up."

Without opening her eyes, Grandma murmured, "Baby girl, after breakfast, I need you to go get Miss Tang and Mrs. Mousa. Tell them to bring the other women, too. We're going to cook our tails off! Tell Mrs. Katz we're going to need some jasmine rice. Tell everyone to bring what they can, and get here right after lunch. I miss our gatherings, and I need my girlfriends."

I hurried to make breakfast—cornmeal porridge—and placed it on the table. I called for my Grandparents, and once we sat down, I told funny stories about things I did when I was little, watching my grandmother laugh with glee at the memories of my antics.

After breakfast, I cleaned up the kitchen and told Grandpa I was off to gather Grandma's girlfriends, letting them know she wanted to cook.

Which meant there'd be a **feast**, a **drinking party**, and **lots of noise**. We hadn't had one of these gatherings since summer, and I was excited to eat well tonight. Grandma must be feeling much better to want to stand up and cook with her girlfriends. No wonder she had such a late start—she had been resting up.

Just as I was about to leave, I turned back to Grandpa and asked, "Grandpa, will there be sweet potato pudding?" Saying the words felt like I was eight years old again.

My grandfather smiled, turned me around, and gave me a pat on the back. "Off you go, child," he said softly, his voice warm and reassuring. There was a tenderness in the gesture, the kind of quiet affection that had been woven into the fabric of their relationship for so many years. "Agnus gets what Agnus wants. That's how I lived my life, with the love of my life." He repeated the words again, this time in a softer tone, "Agnus gets what Agnus wants."

About two hours later, I returned with Kye, carrying several packages that the grand ladies had given to me. I placed the packages in the kitchen and walked with Kye to the backyard, calling out for my grandfather. He and my grandmother were at Mr. Mousa's backyard, where several of the young men of my generation were patiently listening to the elders as they walked them through how to build an earth oven. It seemed that, after all, there would be sweet potato pudding tonight.

The ladies arrived, and it seemed the whole village did as well. Children and grandchildren, relatives, even some of my aunts, uncles, and their children had come. Word had gotten out, and it just kept spreading. The house, both inside and outside, was crowded with people. Everyone was chipping in to cook a feast. There was a pig being roasted, goats being stewed, children playing, men gathered around the dominoes table, and women gossiping.

And there I was, by the earth oven, breathing in the sweet smell of my grandmother's sweet potato pudding. I was older now, a grown woman, with a child of my own. I should be the one making sweet potato pudding for him. But this weekend, Augustus, now six, was with his father, Alan, at a medical conference two parishes over. Alan and I had met where I worked, and we had a whirlwind romance. I knew he was the right person for me when my grandfather took him on a bush walk and he survived.

I found a quiet spot in the yard and gave Alan a call, letting him know all the events of the weekend, and more importantly, that he was going to miss a grand feast and, even more significant, my grandmother's famous sweet potato pudding. I could hear the sigh in his voice and the regret in his words. He promised to wrap up as soon as he could and head back; they should be there by Monday afternoon. I made no promises that any sweet potato pudding would be left for either of them when they returned.

Needless to say, I kept my eye on my grandmother's face as I sat between her and Grandpa. I had dinner and watched how patiently my Grandparents were with each other. They took every opportunity to hug, to smile. It seemed as if their hands were always linked together. Why hadn't I noticed this before? Why hadn't I noticed how much they seemed like one person, how their walking steps matched?

The moments when my grandfather's hands slowly wrapped around my grandmother's waist, or how he seemed to take every opportunity to touch her in some small way, had always been there, but I hadn't noticed. My grandmother always seemed to find Grandpa's eyes, no matter how far away they were from each other. There was always a look, a nod, a smile between them. And more importantly, why was I noticing this now, when I hadn't before?

A deep panic seemed to rise within me. I looked around the backyard, taking in every moment of everyone around me as if in slow motion—trying to memorize their faces, what they were doing, who they were speaking to, how everything smelled. Who was beating the drums? Who was singing? Which child was trying to outdance the other? It felt as if time slowed down as I stood there, drinking in the entire scene.

I walked over to my grandmother, hugged her from behind, and rested my chin upon her shoulder. I placed my mouth right by her ear and whispered, "I love you. I love you more than myself."

Grandma slowly turned around, pulling my forehead to hers. She said softly, "I'm going to need you to love yourself more than you love anyone else. Otherwise, Lorna, I will be disappointed in you. If you don't love yourself, how would you expect anyone else to love you? You must love yourself more than anyone else. That way, you can teach your loved ones how to love, as I have taught you how to love."

She squeezed both my hands, then placed my hands together and gently took me to my grandfather. She took his hands in hers and placed mine within them. She stood there, looking at him with such love and tenderness, then said, the words I pass on to you now, a secret only I now know; "Put a rose in my mouth when it's time, and I will see you both on the other side."

She then started to cough—a cough that didn't seem to stop. Everyone gathered around, concerned. We gently helped her over to her rocking chair that was sitting on the front porch. She sat down, and my grandfather rushed through the kitchen to bring her one of his special brews, one he knew would help her feel better. She thanked him in a soft whisper, drinking the brew.

My grandfather, ever the caretaker, effortlessly lifted her into his arms and walked to their bedroom. I helped him as he laid her down in bed. He shooed me away, telling me to take care of the guests, that he would look after Agnus.

I went to the backyard and told everyone that she was fine, just a little tired, and that they should continue enjoying the evening. We all rallied together, as we always did, packaging up the leftovers, cleaning up, and saying our goodbyes.

I went into my Grandparents' bedroom to check on Grandma. She was asleep, and Grandpa was beside her, slowly brushing her hair with his hands. I went over and kissed his cheek. "Grandpa, are you okay?"

He looked at me with a calm, steady gaze, and replied, "We will be alright." He held my hand and looked into my eyes, repeating, "We will be alright."

I kissed his cheek once more, then whispered, "Goodnight." And I left them there, together, in the quiet of the room.

I woke early, around 3:00 AM, as I felt someone padding my leg. Drowsily, I pushed myself into a sitting position and looked to the end of the bed—it was my grandmother. Her frail, familiar figure stood there, soft light from the early morning creeping around the edges of her form. She smiled at me gently.

"Lorna, take care," she whispered. "Tell everyone I say goodbye. I will tell Esther how well you're doing. Take care of Augustus. He will be fine. Make sure he eats regularly, but don't let him go for walks by himself. Go with him each day for his walks. I know this will be hard, but if you can't go, make sure someone goes with him. We've been walking together since I was sixteen. I don't think he knows how to take his daily walks without me, or Wishes being with him. My baby girl, I will see you on the other side."

I reached my hand out, wanting to touch her, but I felt myself struggling to rise from the bed, attempting to gently reassure her that she was going to be fine. I wanted to walk her back to her bed, but when I looked up—there was no one there. My heart pounded, and I rubbed my eyes, wondering if I had just dreamt about her.

I jumped out of bed, confusion taking hold, and rushed to my Grandparents' room. I knocked on the door. No answer. I knocked again, louder this time. Still no response. My heart began to race, and with growing urgency, I opened the door.

There, on the bed, my grandfather was cradling my grandmother, silently weeping. I rushed over, instinctively slipping into my role as a nurse, checking her vitals. She had passed.

To be honest, I don't remember much of the next 48 hours. People came and went, speaking to me, but it felt like my world had collapsed, with only my grandfather, my son Augustus, and my husband Alan remaining in focus. Their faces and voices were the only things I could recognize in that moment. It felt as though everything else faded. I think I agreed to everything everyone said—whether I heard them or not.

I remember my grandfather, determined and steady, wanting my grandmother to be prepared and dressed for burial according to their traditions. He had a private conversation with the morticians, assuring them that he would take care of Agnes as only he could. They agreed out of respect for him—a man they had known their entire lives, who had watched them grow up.

I went with the grand ladies—to gather flowers. It seemed as if we collected every flower that bloomed that year. The men, alongside my grandfather, gathered herbs. My grandfather carefully washed her body, while I, with great reverence, combed her hair and laid her favorite jewelry on her. He dressed her in a bright yellow dress, the color she loved most.

As he prepared her, my grandfather spoke softly to me. *"Your grandmother's favorite color is yellow, did you know? Her wedding dress was yellow. This is the dress I now put on her."* He paused for a moment, then added, *"She didn't like her nails painted. She didn't care much for wearing a lot of makeup."*

Once he had finished, he covered her and turned to the cotton tree. He asked me to fetch the ladder.

"Grandpa, be careful," I said, hesitating. "Why are you climbing the cotton tree?"

He looked at me, his eyes heavy with emotion. *"I need to do this, for Agnes,"* he said softly. *"Please, hold the ladder still. This may be my last climb up the tree for her."*

Tears began to roll down his face, and I instinctively reached out, touching his hand. "Grandpa, I'll go up," I offered.

"No, baby girl, you can't. I'll show you one day, but right now I have to do this for Agnes."

I watched him, as he slowly climbed the cotton tree, his movements deliberate. He spoke to the tree for what seemed like an eternity—maybe to Agnes, or to some memory shared between them. It felt like time had slowed as I stood below, watching him with deep reverence. After more than thirty minutes, he made his way down, and then asked me to fetch Kye to play the drums for the burial and to have Merry bring fresh honeycomb.

When I returned, the others had gathered. The grand ladies had filled my grandmother's coffin and grave, and the entire yard was filled with followers. My grandfather still stood by her side, speaking little, his world seeming to shrink down to only a few people—me, my grandmother, and their memories.

He stood up and took my hand, leading me to the casket. He bent over, kissed her lips, then opened her mouth and pulled a large, beautiful red rose from his shirt. He placed the flower gently in her mouth, kissed her lips again, and whispered, *"See you in the next life."*

Taking my hand, he led me away from the grave. Confused and emotional, I asked, "Grandpa, why did you do that? Why are we going into the house? Everyone is here for the burial."

He didn't respond immediately, and I had no choice but to follow him as he gently tugged me into the house, down the hallway, and into my Grandparent's bedroom. He told me sternly to sit and listen, and not to interrupt.

"Your grandmother's request was for a rose to be placed in her mouth," he said, his voice steady but filled with sorrow. *"She said she would see me in the next life. I cannot break that bond. I cannot break that promise. I must follow her."*

A deep sense of loss filled the room as he paused, his eyes staring far away, as if lost in a memory only he could see. *"Soon, you'll be here on your own, little one. I've left your great family."*

I couldn't hold back the tears. *"Grandpa, I don't understand…"*

"Little one, I'm preparing you for when I must go to your grandmother," he said softly. *"I can feel it in my soul, and I know it's going to be soon. I'm lost without her. Your eyes are the only thing that grounds me."*

His words hung in the air, heavy with finality. He continued, I'm going to tell you something about your grandmother that no one else knows. Her family immigrated from India. They took care of human waste. She grew up surrounded by the stench of filth until she was 15. When I met her, she was sixteen, and she would do everything she could to cover herself with flowers. She always felt like she could still smell that stench, no matter how clean she was. I made sure she always had flowers around her. I made sure Agnus had whatever Agnus needed. That is why, when she made that last request for a rose to be placed in her mouth, I knew she would be leaving me soon." She was never one to fight against nature, even if it was meant to save her life.

He looked at me with sorrow in his eyes. *"Within six months of arriving in this country, her mother and father both died of the diseases they brought with them, after living in such filth for years. Agnes barely survived. To cure her and save her life. My father buried her up to her neck in a pit in this very backyard. She has been the love of my life ever since. Her devotion to me, to our children, our neighbors, our family—it's unmatched. I don't want her to be alone for too long."* Like how she felt being in that pit; delirious for days; with no family to chant or sing for her. Only the voices of strangers pleading with her to stay as life has a promise of joy to give her. I fell in love with her spirit in those days as I watched   her slowly heal her way back to life. Our souls bonded as we journeyed and I am now breaking from inside out.

He took a deep breath, wiped his face with his sleeve, and stood up. *"I'm going to stay here with you for a while. I need you to show me your strength. But then, I have to go. Your grandmother needs me."*

Grandpa's voice faltered as he spoke again, softer this time, *"Before I go, I will take you to the big cotton tree. I'll tell you one final secret. When I do that, little one, consider it our moment of goodbye."*

As I sat there, the words felt like a final farewell, and a weight settled over me.

What I remember most about my grandmother's funeral wasn't the beautiful songs sung by the village as they carried her coffin to the family graveyard. It wasn't placing her in the ground, filling the grave with flowers. It wasn't even putting the dirt on top of her. What I remember most was **Mr. Katz**, holding my grandfather as he finally broke down and wept like I'd never seen before. What I remembered most was the scream I made. It didn't sound like my voice, but it came from deep within me—filled with rage. I screamed at my grandfather for openly denying me his presence for as long as I wanted it. I was so angry at him for telling me the truth, for showing me the depth of his love for Grandma.

Although I was angry with my grandfather, I was still obsessed with being by his side every minute of the day. I took a leave of absence from work, which allowed me to focus on my time with my husband, Alan, and my son, Augustus. We fell into a steady rhythm over the next year. Every morning, we took long walks together—me and my grandfather—stopping by the grave of my grandmother and the other family members. We'd even visit back by the garden to see **Wishes' grave**. Grandpa would still go over to his friend's house for game night, and I found myself doing as I used to do when I was a child: pulling a stool up beside them and listening to their stories as they played **dominoes**.

One evening, during dinner, my grandfather announced that he wanted to spend some alone time with Alan, my husband. *"Sometimes, men need men's time,"* he had told me when I was a child. So, I took Augustus with me and we went outside under the **big cotton tree**, where I started a fire. We decided to roast some cashews and peanuts, watching the flames dance as the smoke curled into the sky. The soft evening light bathed the backyard in a golden hue, with the sounds of the village—children playing, distant laughter, and the faint beat of drums—faded in the background.

After what seemed like an hour, Alan came to join us. *"Grandpa has retired for the night,"* he said softly.

I looked at him with concern, my worry rising. *"Is he okay? What did you talk about? Is he feeling unwell? Did something happen?"*

Alan reached over and kissed my forehead. *"Augustus is fine,"* he reassured me. *"He just wanted to talk and find out how we were doing."*

It was in that moment that Augustus, now six, looked up with wide, curious eyes. *"Grandpa's name is Augustus, like mine?"*

We both looked at him, surprised. Then I smiled. *"Of course, how did you not know this?"* I said, chuckling softly.

Alan, with his deep and soothing voice, began to sing a lamenting tune—a song about the good times passed, with better times coming ahead. The music wrapped around us like a comforting blanket, soft and warm. Alan, with his quiet demeanor, often found solace in the simple moments of family life. His deep, steady voice always seemed to carry weight, whether he was humming a song or giving a thoughtful response. I knew he respected my grandfather, not just for the wisdom in his eyes but for the quiet strength that he carried even in the most difficult times.

Alan wasn't born into the kind of close, knit, tradition, driven family like what I grew up in. While my roots were deeply embedded in the soil of this land, Alan came from a world where family ties weren't so tightly woven. He was an only child, raised in a city far from the warmth of the countryside, where family dinners weren't filled with lively chatter and stories. But somehow, when he entered my life, he seemed to embrace the role of family member with ease.

The first time he met my grandfather, I was anxious, unsure of how the two would connect. My grandfather had this imposing presence, and though his manner was gentle, he could be a tough nut to crack. I watched with bated breath as Alan shook his hand, sensing my grandfather's steady, appraising gaze. Alan, being the quiet, thoughtful man he is, never flinched. His deep voice, so calm, complemented my grandfather's wisdom in a way that created an unspoken understanding between them.

I always remember that moment—my grandfather, who had never let anyone into the circle of his trust without a test, had invited Alan to join him for a bush walk. It was the ultimate test, as Grandpa had done this only for those he considered worthy of his friendship. As they ventured into the wilds of the woods together, I could see that Allan had passed the test, though Grandpa would never say it aloud. From then on, I noticed a shift in their dynamic—subtle, but real. Grandpa began to treat Allan not just as my husband, but as someone who could sit at the table with the elders, someone who had earned his place in our family.

In the quiet moments of the evenings, after dinner, when the adults were unwinding, I would catch Allan sitting silently, his long fingers tracing the rim of his cup. He didn't speak much, but his silence wasn't uncomfortable. It was a silence that carried weight—a man who had seen much, who had lived his own life before joining our chaotic world of storytellers and traditions. He had grown up in a world where people didn't share stories in the same way. I could see how he learned to adapt, to sit with my grandfather and listen to him and the others, nodding with an understanding that came from years of professional expertise as a doctor but not quite from the land.

I notice how much he respected my grandfather. He didn't just respect his knowledge of the land or his wisdom; he respected the man's ability to endure. He admired the way Grandpa could carry the weight of life's challenges with such grace, and he never shied away from difficult conversations. This was something that did not exist in Allan's family. In his family there were lots of difficult conversations that no one dare to begin. Silence was preferred. Allan had learned to cherish the quiet and the loud, the deep and the simple, in a way that blended well with the rhythms of our life here.

We finished our roasted snacks and went inside for the evening, the warmth of the night lingering in our hearts.

The next morning, I joined Grandpa for his daily walk. The crisp, cool air greeted us as we set off. As we passed by **Mr. Tang's house**, my grandfather paused. *"Mr. Tang isn't feeling well,"* he said. We both knew that Mr. Tang was suffering from a heart condition, and my grandfather often brought him medicine.

We went inside Mr. Tang's home, and I stood by his bedside as my grandfather spoke to him at length. I didn't listen closely; instead, I stepped outside to help Mrs. Tang with some of her chores. She asked how my grandfather was doing, and I told her that we had fallen into a routine. He seemed to be adjusting, but I couldn't help but wonder if he was just humoring me—waiting out the days with a quiet acceptance.

Soon, Christmas arrived, and the entire family gathered, with even more children joining the festivities. Grandpa had now become a **great, grandfather** several times over. Some of these children he was meeting for the first time, like **Heather**, the beautiful 18, month, old girl, and **Georgia**, another chubby, beautiful baby girl, only six months old. He even met **Paul** for the first time, though Paul was four years old—his family had traveled often internationally and missed many family gatherings.

Grandpa seemed to want to spend as much time with every single child that Christmas—learning their names, memorizing their faces, and sharing every bit of wisdom he could offer. During our grand Christmas event, story time seemed to stretch on for hours, with what felt like fifty stories being told. Grandpa shared as many stories as he could remember, and the other elders took their turns as well. It was as if this gathering, this **oral history of our family**, was necessary. Every elder passed on the legacy of our past to the children, making sure that they knew the stories that shaped us all.

When everyone had packed up and returned home for their own New Year's celebrations, the house quieted again. We fell back into our regular routine. On New Year's Day, Grandpa woke early and fixed breakfast for everyone. I was always amazed at how strong and mobile he was at such an old age. After breakfast, he announced that he was going on a bush walk with Augustus.

He looked at Alan and declared, *"You should carry the basket."* My husband readily agreed, and they all left me at home. No one asked if I wanted to go, and I think I was excluded because I'd lost my common sense, as I had when I was younger, and common sense was necessary for such treks.

No matter—I busied myself around the house, doing chores, cleaning, folding laundry, and prepping for dinner. Just before sunset, they returned. Augustus' face was sticky with honey, and I knew instantly that he'd been exposed to an experience much like the ones I had around his age. There were no words needed between us. I simply looked at my grandfather, kissed his forehead, and walked Augustus into the bathroom for a quick shower.

For dinner that night, I had outdone myself. I made **curry goat with rice and peas**, a dish that brought the house alive with its spicy, fragrant aromas. All three of us ate with gusto. My grandfather even licked his fingers, which made me smile. He looked at me, pride in his eyes, and declared, *"You cook almost as good as your grandmother."*

Alan and Augustus cleared the table and began cleaning the kitchen. My grandfather motioned for me to come with him to the backyard, under the big, beautiful cotton tree where we all had sat together. We sat down on the grass, and Grandpa spoke in a voice that was soft, almost nostalgic.

"When your grandmother was pregnant with your mother," he began, *"she had me plant those rose bushes over there, on that side of the house. She would go out and pick roses, bringing them back into the house. But as her stomach grew, she would lean over to pick them, and the thorns would scratch her stomach."* He paused for a moment, and I could hear the weight in his voice. *"I insisted she stop doing that, so I would pick the roses for her. One day, I came home, and she was sitting in the bathroom, with brand new scratches on her arms and on her swollen stomach. I was angry, and I went out into the garden. I pulled up every single one of those rose bushes and burned them. I was so angry. Even though I knew how important those bushes were to her, I felt immense remorse as soon as I set them ablaze."*

Grandpa took a deep breath, his voice barely a whisper now. *"Your Grandma didn't speak to me for three days. I thought I had lost my mind. I knelt in front of her, begging for her forgiveness. I did chores she hadn't asked me to do, and I didn't even think she knew I had done them. After two weeks, she came to me. I found a rose bush in the forest, near Butterman's Cliff. You know the place."*

I nodded, remembering. Grandpa continued, *"I dug up that rose bush and kept it alive in a bucket for as long as I could. I didn't know what to do with it, but I cut some of the roses and gave them to your Grandma , placing them by her bedside. I hoped she would forgive me, and she did. After two weeks, your mom joined us. The excitement in the house was unimaginable. This beautiful baby—your mother—joined our family."* As you know we had several more children, your uncles but she was our only girl.

He stood up, brushing the grass from his clothes. *"This tree holds a secret—a gift I gave to your grandmother. Go fetch the ladder, and we'll climb this tree for the last time together. I'm going to show you the secret and pass on the responsibility to you. Once we finish our climb, I will have fulfilled my promise to you."*

After we climbed down the tree, we went together to put away the ladder. I was still in awe, at what I saw up high in the big cotton tree. Grandpa continued to speak to me softly, I could feel my heart heavy with the weight of his words. The tears began to fall silently down my face. *"Lorna, this land is as much a part of us as our blood,"* he said, his voice thick with emotion. *"You may not always see it, but it's alive, just like us. Take care of it, and it will take care of you."*

"Remember, the earth gives, and the earth takes. But it's what you give back to it that matters." As he reached the end of his days, he sought comfort in knowing that the legacy of his teachings would live on. Grandpa held me, walking me back to the house. He kissed me, whispered goodnight, and hugged Augustus tightly. He walked into his bedroom to be with my grandmother, and with one last whispered farewell, he wished himself into passing—from this life to the next.

Merry is her most determined voiced yelled out what was in the tree? What did you see? Lorna stood up walked over to Merry lifted her in her arms and announce that she and everyone would find out in the next story.

"Did he really just go to sleep and die?" Agustus asked, his voice heavy with disbelief. His eyes, wide and filled with questions, searched mine, unsure whether such a thing could be real.

I nodded slowly, feeling the weight of the moment settle over me. *"Yes,"* I replied softly, my voice thick with the truth of it. *"His need to see Agnes again, to be with her, was greater than his need to take another breath."*

I could see the questions flicker in Agustus' eyes, the wonder of a young man yet to fall in love battling with the complexity of love and loss. Was it possible for someone to love so deeply, so unconditionally, that it would transcend even the physical need to survive? Or was I simply telling him a tale of lore—an exaggerated story from the past, something that couldn't possibly be true?

Before I could answer the unspoken question in his gaze, a familiar voice broke through the stillness of the moment. My father, Agustus' grandfather, appeared on the porch, carrying a basket of apples for the children. His steps were firm and steady, a contrast to the grief that still hung in the air, as though he was providing something solid, something nourishing, in the face of uncertainty. He held the basket high, the apples inside gleaming like small suns in the fading light of the afternoon.

"Every word is true," my father said in a loud, clear voice, his tone carrying both authority and warmth. He glanced at Agustus, offering him one of the apples with a soft smile. *"You see, Agustus and Agnes inhaled and exhaled together, at the same rate and pace, even when they weren't near each other. It happened without them even thinking about it. It was a bond that tied them, a connection stronger than anything physical. It began when she was very sick, when she was sixteen, and he stayed by her side, chanting and breathing with her for days as she fought for her life."*

He paused, looking at the children, who were now gathering around him, eager for the apples. His voice softened, but the weight of his words remained. *"That bond, that deep connection they shared, never left them even when Agnes passed on. And it's that love, that unwavering commitment, that carried him to where she is now."*

With that, he handed the apples to the children, one by one. As they took them from his hands, he continued, *"Everyone, come get an apple, and remember to continue being on your best behavior. Your Grandparents, your great, Grandparents, they didn't just teach us about love. They showed us what it meant to live with purpose, to live for each other."*

The children, some of them quietly nibbling on their apples, looked up at my father with wide eyes, taking in his words. They might not have fully understood the depth of what he said, but they understood the weight he placed on those moments—the connection between life and death, love and loss.

As I watched them, I realized that even in their innocence, they were witnessing something profound. The stories of our family—of **Agustus** and **Agnes**, of their timeless bond—were being passed down, one generation to the next. And for a brief moment, the sadness lifted, replaced by the quiet power of shared memory, of family, and of the love that transcended time.

Chapter 9 – Love With Earth & Time

The last story I'll share is about your great, Grandparents," she began. "They weren't just Grandparents. They were the heart of this family. Your great-grandfather's grandpa built this house with his own two hands. Your great, grandfather, Grandpa, worked the fields, but he also built the walls of this home with love. My Grandpa and Grandma made sure that every meal was prepared with care, every room filled with warmth. They were a team, just like all of us."

She paused for a moment, letting the children digest her words. They could sense the reverence in her voice when she spoke of her Grandparents. It wasn't just the house she cherished, but everything it represented—the love, the labor, and the sense of belonging.

"As we sit here now," she continued, her tone more reflective, "we're carrying on their legacy. Every year, we gather under this tree, just like they did. And those of you who are younger, well, you'll carry this tradition too. We're all connected, one generation to the next."

"Gather 'round, children," Lorna began, her voice full of warmth and authority. "I'm going to tell you a story—a secret, really, about your great, grandfather. The big cotton tree you see here… it holds a piece of our family's love and history. And I'm the only one left who knows the whole story."

The children leaned in, intrigued. Lorna's gaze moved slowly over them, her heart swelling with a quiet pride. They were her nieces, nephews, and the youngest of the cousins—great, grandchildren of her grandfather. They were young, full of wonder, and they looked up to her for the stories of the past, just as she had looked up to her Grandparents all those years ago.

"You see, your grandfather, the man we all loved so dearly, had a secret," Lorna continued, her tone lowering as if sharing something sacred. "This tree was planted by his father my great grandfather as a wedding gift to his wife Josephine. My grandfather added something special to this tree for his wife Agnus my grandmother. This tree, it isn't just any tree. It held something more —a rose bush grafted into its trunk, by my grandfather a gift he gave to your great, grandmother on the day their first child was born, my mother Ester."

The children's eyes widened in curiosity, and Lorna felt a soft tug of nostalgia. The love she had witnessed between her Grandparents had always been palpable, like the tree itself—strong, enduring, and deep.

"Your great, grandfather grafted a rose bush into the tree," she said, her voice filled with reverence, "and every year, when the roses bloom, they're for your great, grandmother. It was his way of saying, 'I love you,' a symbol of their bond. And he took care of that rose bush as long as he could, high up in the tree. Only he could climb up and tend to it, and when he could no longer do so, he passed on that responsibility to me."

The children sat in rapt silence, as Lorna's eyes softened with the memory of her grandfather's careful hands working on the bush.

"I never told anyone about the secret of that rose bush until now," she said, a gentle smile tugging at the corners of her lips. "It was something only he and I shared. And I promised him I would take care of it, just as he had, even when he was gone."

Lorna paused, feeling the weight of those promises and the years spent tending to the bush, now hidden high in the cotton tree. "The roses, when they bloom, are fragrant and beautiful. Your great, grandfather always made sure your great, grandmother would receive them as a reminder of his love. And now, every time they bloom, I place them on their graves to keep the promise I made."

The children looked up at her, their faces filled with the same quiet reverence. "So, the roses are for Great, Grandma?" one of the younger children asked, his voice soft.

Lorna nodded; her heart full. "Yes, they are for her. And now, I'm asking for your help. You see, I'm getting older, and it's hard for me to climb the tree like I used to. But I want to make sure this tradition continues. I need someone to help me keep the rose bush alive for future generations, so that you'll know the love your great, grandfather had for your great, grandmother."

Lorna turned to her son, Agustus, who had been quietly listening. He was a young man now, full of promise and ambition, but in this moment, he was still the boy who had run through these fields, playing in the shadow of the cotton tree.

"Agustus," Lorna called gently, "I need your help with this."

Agustus looked up from the group of younger children, his eyes steady, though there was a flicker of emotion in them. He had grown up with this land, and though he had not yet asked all the questions about the past, he understood the importance of what his mother was asking.

"Of course, Mom," he replied, walking over to her. He knelt beside her, his hand resting on hers. "I'll take care of it. Just like Grandpa would've wanted."

Lorna smiled, feeling a deep sense of relief. She had known, without a doubt, that he would say yes. He understood. The legacy of her Grandparents was in him too, and now, he would carry it forward.

"I'm trusting you with this," she said, her voice thick with emotion. "The rose bush is more than just a plant. It's part of our family's heart. It's love that's been passed down through generations. I want you to look after it, for Grandma, for Grandpa, for all of us."

Agustus nodded; his expression thoughtful. "I'll make sure it's taken care of, Mom."

Lorna looked around at the children gathered beneath the cotton tree, feeling the weight of tradition settle over her. She had kept this secret for so long, and now, it was time for the younger generation to carry it forward.

As the roses bloomed in the seasons to come, they would not only be a symbol of her grandfather's love for her grandmother but also a testament to the continuing legacy of their family—a legacy that would be kept alive, generation after generation, by Agustus and the children who had gathered around her today.

The children, still wide-eyed and eager for more, looked up at Lorna with the kind of curiosity that only the young can possess. They had listened intently, but now that the story was told, their minds were full of questions. The oldest of the group, a boy about 10 years old, raised his hand.

"Where is the rose bush?" he asked, his voice filled with wonder. "How come we've never seen it? I mean, we see the tree all the time. Why don't we ever see the roses?"

Lorna smiled softly, her gaze flickering over the children as they looked up at her expectantly. They weren't just hearing about the secret anymore—they were now part of it, part of the tradition. She had shared the story, but now, they wanted proof.

"Ah, I see," Lorna said, a playful twinkle in her eye. "Well, I suppose if you're going to believe the story, you need to see it for yourselves, don't you?"

The children nodded eagerly, their faces lighting up with excitement.

She looked toward Agustus, who had been listening quietly from the edge of the group. The solemn expression on his face told her that the story had struck him just as deeply as it had struck her when her grandfather had first entrusted her with the secret.

"Agustus," she called, her voice full of authority, yet tinged with the warmth of a mother's love. "You know where the ladder is, don't you?"

He nodded slowly, but there was a look of curiosity in his eyes. "You really want me to go up there?" he asked, a little unsure. He had never heard of the rose bush before today. It had been a secret that had stayed with Lorna and her Grandparents.

"Of course," Lorna said, a smile tugging at her lips. "And I want you to take a picture so the children can see what it looks like, and, of course, bring back a rose for them to see." She paused, glancing around at the eager faces of the younger children. "It will be a piece of their history—proof of the love that built this family."

Agustus hesitated for a moment, the weight of her request sinking in. This wasn't just about retrieving a rose; it was about carrying out a family legacy. He had never known the true importance of the rose bush until now. And now, standing under the big cotton tree, a tree he had grown up with, he was about to reconnect with a piece of his great, Grandparents' love.

"Alright," he said with a determined nod, though his curiosity was palpable. "I'll get the ladder."

He walked over to the side of the yard, where the old wooden ladder rested against the shed, a tool of many years, worn and weathered but still sturdy enough for the job. The sunlight glinted off its rough wood as he carried it over to the tree, positioning it against the trunk.

As he set the ladder up, Lorna watched from below, her heart swelling with pride. Agustus had always been a good son—respectful, kind, and thoughtful—but now, with the weight of family history resting on his shoulders, she could see the quiet sense of responsibility that had come over him. This wasn't just about him anymore; it was about ensuring that this tradition carried on for generations.

"Just remember," Lorna called up to him as he began to climb, "the rose bush is high in the tree, near the thickest branch. It's hidden away where not many people can see it. You'll need to be careful, and once you're up there, look for the cluster of roses near the trunk. They're hard to find, but they're worth the effort."

Agustus nodded, climbing higher, his focus sharpened. The ladder creaked beneath him, and he paused, looking back down at Lorna. She was steady, watching him with an intensity that showed how deeply this act meant to her. She wasn't just asking him to get a rose. She was asking him to preserve the love, the promise, and the family bond that had existed long before he was born.

"Got it," he called down, his voice steady. "I think I see it. There's a small cluster near the branch just above the split."

Lorna smiled and waited patiently as Agustus continued climbing. Her thoughts drifted to her Grandparents, to the love they had shared and to the countless hours she had spent as a child learning from them. Her grandfather had cared for that rose bush with the same tenderness he had shown her as he taught her how to care for the things that mattered most—family, love, and tradition.

Agustus finally reached the top of the ladder and carefully peered into the thick foliage. His eyes scanned the trunk of the cotton tree, searching for the elusive flowers. For a long moment, there was silence, the rustling of the leaves in the wind filling the space.

"Ah, here it is!" Agustus called down; his voice filled with awe. "I see the roses now—just like you said. They're nestled right in the crook of the tree. They're beautiful, Mom. I can't believe I've never seen them before."

Lorna's heart swelled. The roses were more than just a physical flower to her; they were a symbol of everything that had been passed down through the family. She had kept them alive in spirit, tending to them in the ways her grandfather had taught her, but now, for the first time, Agustus was seeing them too.

"Take a picture," Lorna instructed, her voice quiet but firm, "and make sure you pick one. Just one, for the children."

Agustus carefully plucked a single, delicate rose from the bush, its petals soft and velvety in his hand. He held it up to the light, the rose's deep red color glowing in the sun. The air around him seemed to hush as he took a moment to admire it, then he carefully wrapped it in a piece of cloth from his pocket to protect it for the descent. He then carefully took his phone out of his pocket and snap a picture of the rose bush nestled in the tree.

"Alright, I'm coming down," he said, carefully making his way down the ladder with the rose in hand and the camera ready for a picture.

When he reached the ground, he handed the rose to Lorna, his face filled with wonder.

"The bush really does bloom," he said softly. "It's incredible. It's like something out of a fairy tale."

Lorna took the rose from his hands, her fingers brushing against his as she received it. She smiled, feeling a quiet satisfaction in her heart.

"Your great, grandfather's love for your great, grandmother is in this rose," she said, looking down at it. "This bush has lived on because of their love—and now, it's your turn to help care for it."

Agustus nodded slowly, the weight of her words settling in. He had just connected with something deeper than he had expected. This was no longer just about a graduation weekend. This was about his place in the long line of family history, and he now carried that responsibility forward.

Lorna handed the rose to one of the children, who took it eagerly. The other children crowded around, peering at the flower, which now symbolized the deep love and tradition they were inheriting.

"Now you know," Lorna said, "that this is our family's heart. And with Agustus helping me, we'll keep it alive, just as Grandpa did, and as I have done for all these years."

As Agustus handed the rose to one of the children, Lorna watched the group of eager faces surrounding it. The air seemed to buzz with excitement, and a slow realization began to dawn on the children. Their wide-eyes shifted between Lorna, the rose, and each other. It was as if the weight of the story had truly settled into their young minds. They weren't just hearing a tale—they were witnessing a living piece of their family's history.

One of the younger girls, no older than seven, gasped and whispered, "It's real! The bush is real!"

Another child, slightly older, leaned in, her voice quivering with excitement, "So, it's true? All of it? The tree… and the rose… Grandpa really did that for Grandma?"

Lorna smiled; her heart warmed by their wonder. "Yes," she said, her voice soft but firm. "The bush is real, and everything I've told you is true. The love your great, grandfather had for your great, grandmother lives on through that tree and the roses. And now you're part of that history too."

There was a long, stunned silence, and then, almost in synchronized chaos, the children began to scramble to their feet, their eyes wide with amazement. The youngest of them, a boy of about nine, turned to the others and shouted, "We have to tell our parents! We have to tell them what we saw!"

The others, equally as excited, began running toward the Great Hall, their voices rising in a chorus. "The rose bush! We saw it! It's real! It's in the tree!"

The adults, who had been relaxing after lunch and catching up on old stories, looked up in confusion as the children burst into the room, nearly tripping over themselves in their excitement. The adults exchanged puzzled glances.

"What in the world is all this commotion about?" Uncle Marley asked, his voice half, laughing, half, curious.

"It's true! It's really true!" one of the children exclaimed, barely able to catch his breath.

Another child, eager to explain, began, "There's a rose bush grafted into the cotton tree! Great-Grandpa did it for Great-Grandma on the day Ester was born! And it's still there! We saw it with our own eyes!"

For a moment, the room was filled with disbelief and surprise. The adults exchanged skeptical glances, unsure of what to make of the children's frantic words. But when Agustus entered the room, holding his phone which showed the picture he had taken of the rose bush in the tree and the rose carefully wrapped in cloth, the children's story suddenly gained weight.

Agustus walked to the front of the room and held up his phone with the photo for everyone to see. "It's true," he said, his voice calm but filled with awe. "I climbed the tree, just like Mom said. I found the rose bush, and I took a picture. We all need to go see it."

The room fell silent as the weight of Agustus' words settled in. The elders who had been skeptical now stood up one by one, exchanging looks of astonishment. Without another word, several of them began heading toward the backyard, eager to see the legendary rose bush for themselves.

As the day turned to evening, the elders who could still climb—and even those who couldn't but were determined—had gathered under the cotton tree. One by one, they climbed the ladder or took to the branches, carefully making their way to the hidden rose bush. The children hovered nearby, eager to witness this moment of wonder, their excitement palpable.

Lorna stood near the base of the tree, her arms crossed, watching the family as they took turns gazing at the secret her grandfather had kept for so long. The scene felt almost surreal. What had started as a simple story now had a physical presence, a piece of family history that was being passed down to every generation.

After a few hours, the last of the elders climbed down, each of them with a sense of reverence in their eyes. They had seen the roses—each of them, in their own way, had connected with the legacy of Lorna's Grandparents. The love they shared was now visible to all, as if it had always been waiting for them to see it.

"We swear," Uncle Joseph said, his voice deep and serious, "we will take care of this rose bush. We will keep it alive, just as your grandfather did. And we will keep the secret in the family."

The other elders nodded in agreement, some with their hands over their hearts, others placing a hand on the tree trunk in solemnity. They had witnessed the love that had endured through the years, and now they understood the weight of their responsibility.

Lorna watched them, her eyes misting over with emotion. This was a moment she would never forget—a moment where her Grandparents' legacy had been passed from one generation to the next, where the family had sworn an oath to keep the love alive.

My Grandparents were not here to see this moment, but I could feel their presence. I could almost hear my grandfather's voice, reminding me to cherish these moments with my family, to carry on the traditions he had instilled in me. His absence was a quiet ache, but one softened by the laughter around me, by the new generation carrying on the stories. It made me realize how much I had learned from him and how much I was now passing down to Agustus, just as he had once done for me.

As the sun dipped below the horizon and the family made their way back to the house, Lorna felt a deep sense of fulfillment. The air was cool now, and the laughter of the younger children had faded into the soft hum of nightfall. Over the next two hours cars were filled with luggage, lots of photos were taken, gifts exchanged and goodbye rituals were expressed amongst the family members with promises to return for more visits.

With a quite hush now spreading over the property. Lorna with Agustus walking beside her made their way to the family graveyard, a short walk down the path from the house. Lorna had always felt a strong connection to this place, where her Grandparents lay side by side. Tonight, as she approached the graves, she felt the weight of her family's history and love pressing down on her. She reached out, gently brushing the soft grass near her grandfather's headstone, then placing the single rose Augustus had brought down from the tree onto her grandmother's grave.

Agustus stood beside her, his hands shoved deep into his pockets, his eyes thoughtful. "I still can't believe it," he said quietly. "The rose bush was there all these years, and I never knew."

"I've kept the secret, just as Grandpa wanted," Lorna said softly, her voice thick with emotion. "But now, I'm getting older, and I can't care for it the way I used to. I needed to share it with the family, to make sure it lives on. And now, you will help me, Agustus. You'll help keep the love alive for future generations."

She stood there for a long moment, her heart heavy with the sense of finality, yet also filled with love for the family she had grown up in. "I've kept my promise, Grandma, Grandpa," she whispered to the graves, "but the world has changed, and I can't do it alone anymore. I've passed on the secret, and I know you'd be proud of what we've done today."

Agustus, standing quietly beside her, nodded slowly. "We'll keep it alive mom. Just like you said. We won't let it die."

Lorna smiled, her eyes welling with tears. "Thank you," she whispered, her voice filled with a mix of relief and love. As the two of them stood in silence, the stars began to twinkle above, and Lorna felt a quiet peace settle in her heart. The legacy of love and family that had been passed down to her would now be carried forward, not just by her son, but by the whole family.

The house, now back to its familiar state of inhabitance, seemed to exhale with Lorna as she sat on the front porch in her grandmother's rocking chair. The warm evening air wrapped around her like a blanket, carrying the scent of earth and distant wood smoke from the neighboring homes. Alan sat beside her in her grandfather's rocking chair, the one that had witnessed decades of quiet moments and heavy conversations. They sipped the mint tea that Agustus had carefully brought them, its coolness mingling with the warmth of the evening.

Together, they waved goodbye to their son as he left with his friends for a night of fun. His youthful energy filled the space before he disappeared into the night, leaving behind a hushed, almost sacred silence.

For several minutes, neither spoke. The sound of crickets chirping and the rustling of leaves in the trees filled the air. Lorna leaned back in the chair, letting the stillness wash over her. It was the kind of quiet that only came after an eventful day, when the weight of shared stories and emotions hung in the air, waiting to settle.

Finally, Alan spoke, his voice low and soft, echoing the cadence of her grandfather's voice—a voice that Lorna had heard so many times throughout her life, full of quiet strength. *"Na Na,"* Alan's nickname for her, a word of affection laced with familiarity. *"Are you okay?"*

Lorna let out a low grunt, a sound that served as her only response, signaling that she wasn't quite ready to break the silence.

Alan tried again, his gaze steady, turning to face her more directly now. *"Seems like you had a lot of secrets to share with the entire family,"* he said, his tone gentle but carrying the weight of the question.

Once more, Lorna grunted in affirmation, her lips pressed together as though she were trying to hold back a tide of words. She could feel the weight of his words, the heaviness of unspoken truths between them.

Without another word, Alan stood up, his movements quiet and deliberate. He reached for her tea cup, taking it from her hands without asking, and made his way into the kitchen. The sound of the cups being washed—clinking gently in the sink—seemed to punctuate the space between them, marking the separation of thought, of words left unsaid. When the cups were clean, he left the kitchen and headed toward their bedroom—the room that had once been shared by her Grandparents. The door creaked as it closed softly behind him.

Lorna remained sitting on the porch, her eyes fixed on the fading light of day. She didn't move as the minutes turned to hours, as the last of the sun dipped below the horizon and the fireflies began their slow dance in the cool night air. The faint hoot of an owl warned the other creatures of the dark to stay away, and the night seemed to embrace her in its cool quiet.

The world around her continued to breathe—nightfall came and the stars emerged, the sky a blanket of dark velvet with scattered pinpricks of light. Yet, in this silence, Lorna's heart felt heavy. The stories she had shared, the truths she had uncovered, were still pressing on her soul. The secrets that she had kept for so long, the parts of her life that she had hidden—even from Alan—felt like a weight she could no longer bear.

In our early years together, I often wondered if Allan would ever truly understand my connection to the farm, to the traditions that had shaped me. At first, he would joke about his unfamiliarity with the land—how it felt strange to be surrounded by so much quiet, so much history. Yet, as time passed, I saw how much he grew to respect the old ways, how he started to appreciate the simplicity of our life, even in its complexity. He learned how to appreciate the rhythm of farm life: the steady pace of the seasons, the joy in shared meals, and the connection to the land.

But what struck me most about Allan was his ability to listen, really listen, to my grandfather's stories. Unlike some, who would nod politely or only half, listen, Allan was fully engaged. He asked questions, not to show off his knowledge, but because he genuinely wanted to understand. When Grandpa spoke about his past, about the hardships he had faced, Allan's respect was palpable. There was something about the way he absorbed the weight of Grandpa's words that made me love him even more.

Allan's sense of family had evolved since we married. Initially, his world was built on self, sufficiency—his small, tightknit relationship with his parents and close friends. But when we moved back to the farm, I saw him develop a deeper, more expansive sense of family. He became deeply connected to my Grandparents, particularly Grandpa, who welcomed him with open arms.

Over the years, Allan grew to value not just the farm's physical beauty, but the sense of legacy that lived within its soil. He often took long walks by himself, sometimes with Augustus, reflecting on his own childhood, trying to find parallels between his urban upbringing and the way our family lived. But the more he reflected, the more he saw that family wasn't just about shared blood—it was about shared experiences. And he embraced it fully. He's not one for loud displays, but there's a certain satisfaction in his eyes when he watches our son navigate the world—just as I watched him navigate his first years with my family. I sometimes catch him smiling at Agustus, seeing a reflection of my grandfather in him, as though he, too, had inherited some of the patience and wisdom Grandpa always carried with him.

Finally, she let out a long, slow sigh. It was a breath that seemed to release the tension from her bones. She rose from the chair, the creaking of the wood beneath her a quiet sound against the deep silence of the night. She walked toward the house, her mind racing with thoughts, with the promises she had made to herself and to the ones she loved. She would face the truth tomorrow—just as she had done in the past.

She took a long, cleansing bath, the warm water soothing her aching muscles and stilling her mind. When she stepped out of the water, she could feel the weight of the night on her shoulders. She dressed slowly, the silence of the house around her broken only by the soft sounds of her movements.

As she climbed into bed, her mind was still turning, but her body was exhausted. She closed her eyes, knowing that when dawn broke, she would face Alan. She would look him in the eye, apologize for the secrets she had kept, only to then share them in such a manner with the family without regard for his feelings. She would then promise him to live the life of love and respect that her ancestors had passed down to her.

Tomorrow, she would give him the best apology she could muster and as he deserved. She would apologize as she had learnt how to do when she was eight from her grandfather after he gave away her giant pumpkin. Yes, she would square her shoulders look him in the eye and state we are one and you should have been told first about the rose bush in the tree. I am sorry. With that thought, she hoped to begin again. As the first light of dawn peeked through the curtains, Lorna drifted to sleep, her heart quiet for the moment, knowing that the road ahead would require strength, honesty, and a willingness to heal.

The End for now.

www.ingramcontent.com/pod-product-compliance
Lightning Source LLC
Chambersburg PA
CBHW052131030426
42337CB00028B/5122